# WHAT YOU KNOW ABOUT
# STARTUPS IS WRONG

# What you know about startups*

# *is wrong

HOW TO NAVIGATE ENTREPRENEURIAL URBAN LEGENDS
THAT THREATEN YOUR RELATIONSHIPS,
YOUR HEALTH, YOUR FINANCES, AND YOUR CAREER

KP Reddy

**LIONCREST**
PUBLISHING

WHAT YOU KNOW ABOUT STARTUPS IS WRONG

*How to Navigate Entrepreneurial Urban Legends That Threaten
Your Relationships, Your Health, Your Finances, and Your Career*

ISBN   978-1-61961-879-4 *Paperback*
　　　 978-1-61961-878-7 *Ebook*

# Contents

---

# Foreword

*By James Andrews*

———

Walking the earth as an entrepreneur is like being a lonely planet, and most people find startup founders to be nuts. Thank God for K.P. Reddy. He's part investor, part guru, part entrepreneur and for many, including myself, he's a founder's founder. What K.P. prescribes in *What You Know About Startups Is Wrong* is the recipe and blueprint we have all been looking for. The chapters represent all the things business schools should be teaching and your father never taught you. Delivered in the unmistakable K.P. Reddy voice, this book should be required reading for anyone crazy enough to consider a startup and wise enough to seek the right counsel. Do yourself a favor and get as close as you can to K.P. Reddy and the principles he discusses in this book; you can thank me later.

—JAMES ANDREWS, FOUNDER/MANAGING PARTNER, AUTHENTIC VENTURES

# Introduction

—

The first time I got a raise, I was twenty-two and working as a civil engineer for Law Engineering, a firm in Atlanta. After a year, the company informed everyone that depending on our performance, we would receive a 3 to 6 percent salary increase from a bonus pool. When I found out I had hit the top band—6 percent—I was thrilled. Until I opened up my paycheck. I was making $28,000 a year. Six percent, I saw, was roughly $1,600. After taxes, it wasn't enough to purchase anything big like a new car.

I felt screwed over. I had done what I had been told to do: Be a great engineer. Work on great projects. Build technical credibility. Now, I was being acknowledged with the top salary increase—but what did it all mean? What had been the point of working so hard? I could have shown up, done an OK job, gotten a 4 percent increase, and there wouldn't have been much difference in my paycheck. I ran a spreadsheet calculating what I'd earn if I hit the 6 percent increase for the next ten years, and I realized it wasn't that much money. It wasn't bad money, but I didn't know if I'd ever be able to afford a house. I couldn't see the path.

Very few people I know are content with their jobs and incomes. Many feel limited, even trapped, creatively and financially. That's what drives the dream of being an entrepreneur. Another driver is, out in the world, we're often defined by our job descriptions—but if we're doing work we don't like, and our companies won't let us expand, we feel diminished. Many people mistakenly believe a job description defines who they are. If their jobs suck, maybe they do, too.

Sometimes, we get on a treadmill of getting new jobs and new salaries to create a new sense of ourselves. When that doesn't work, people often buy into a fundamental belief that because they're unhappy in the traditional world of work, they're cut out to be entrepreneurs. They buy into this without knowing the costs and the reality of the road ahead.

## THE NEW BATMANS

Entrepreneurs are the new superheroes (without the tights, of course). We know their origin stories by heart: Bill

Gates dropped out of Harvard to start Microsoft. Steve Jobs started Apple in his parents' garage. Mark Zuckerberg began Facebook in his dorm room, fueled by Hot Pockets. When I was growing up, my friends and I looked up to athletes like Michael Jordan, amazed by his slam dunks. Today, I've got a seventeen-year-old and fifteen-year-old son who keep up with people like billionaire entrepreneur Elon Musk, the co-founder of Tesla and SpaceX. They're enamored with his efforts to change the world through electric cars and space travel, with his belief that online gaming will ultimately create a Matrix-like existence.

The stories of superhero tech billionaires all have a compelling and familiar trajectory: an outsider puts everything on the line for a dream. By doing so, he wins big and changes the universe. Musk is an immigrant born in South Africa who started writing code when he was around ten years old. He dropped out of Stanford and scored millions in the dot-com era by selling his company to PayPal. But instead of stopping there, he kept going. It would have been easy for Musk to start another successful payment company like Venmo. Instead, he went on to do things totally outside of his comfort zone, risking his professional reputation and telling everyone we need to colonize Mars.

## THE LEGEND

The mainstream news is jam-packed with stories of entrepreneurial risk-takers like Musk. As a result, the number one urban legend about being an entrepreneur today is anybody can be one. A huge startup culture feeds that myth with classes, books, podcasts, coaching, university degrees, certifications, and mastermind groups. Pithy, cool, and cursing motivational speakers on entrepreneurship are everywhere (but many have never been real entrepreneurs themselves). Inundated with stories of entrepreneurs who dropped out of college and got a second mortgage to make their dream a reality, people believe success can be willed. They hold onto tales like that of FedEx founder Fred Smith. When Smith couldn't pay the company's fuel bill, he took the company's last $5,000 and hopped on a plane to Las Vegas. He won $27,000 playing blackjack and saved FedEx from going under.

Start-up entrepreneurs are the new rock stars. It used to be, if you were a well-known musician or music producer, waiters and waitresses would press their demo tapes on you everywhere you went. Today, if you're a successful entrepreneur, the baristas at Starbucks slide over to your table and ask you to take a look at their business plans. I have a lot of friends in the music industry where I live in Atlanta— mostly in hip-hop and rap. One of them is a star-maker, but he jokes with me that as an entrepreneur, I get recognized and hit up for advice around town more than he does.

Many of the ideas I get asked about are a result of people's obsession with the reality show *Shark Tank*. One woman came to me with the idea of selling sheets with Velcro attached to the bottom so your top sheet won't slip off the bed. I told her it wasn't going to fly, because people could just buy Velcro and iron it on themselves. She argued no one was doing that, nor were they going to. I said if they weren't doing it, then maybe wayward top sheets weren't a huge problem that needed a solution. Another guy pitched me an app that lets you share your dog with people who want to borrow it for companionship. "The Uber of pets," he called it. I didn't see how he'd make money. Plus, are pet owners really going to let strangers borrow their dogs for the afternoon? I'm not sure about that...or whether *Shark Tank* is the best guide for learning how to be a successful entrepreneur.

## THE TRUTH

I think that being an entrepreneur is probably one of the hardest things anyone can do on a personal level. You never hear about the people who gambled on payroll but lost. Everyone says the number one trait a start-up entrepreneur needs to have is perseverance. I don't think so. The number one trait is knowing when to quit and when to move on, because sometimes there's a reason why plans aren't working. That's what you have to spend your time analyzing. I'm not the ultimate authority, but I have had the experience of winning and losing in the startup world. There are plenty of books out there telling you how to build your business model, but my hope with this one is to talk about the human factor.

Underneath the fairy tales about entrepreneurs living on no sleep and eating Beanee Weenees for a year are harsher realities. Startup pressures lead to people losing their homes, their health, and often, their marriages. I met an entrepreneur once who had left his wife and kids behind in Ukraine to co-found a startup in the United States. He hadn't seen his family for a year and a half. Leaving them behind was one of his selling points to investors as he insisted this proved how committed he was. Any situation where you're not there for your family is considered a good thing is going too far. Investors perpetuate the cycle with take-no-prisoners expectations. They push founders into believing extreme sacrifices are required.

As a result, you often hear investors say, "I'm betting on the jockey, not the horse." When they see an entrepreneur willing to go to any lengths, they (mistakenly) figure he or she must have the guts to make a success happen, if not with their current company then the next. Countless investors fail to focus on the substance of an idea or business model, or the strength of a market and how to approach it. They don't see the reality that a business is a commodity that needs cash and investments as resources to fuel it. Getting underneath the hood and figuring out how the thing is going to run is critical—especially because it might not run at all. Instead, investors say to an entrepreneur, "I like your idea. More importantly, I like you. You're a go-getter." What entrepreneurs hear from comments like these is aggressiveness is more important than a substantive idea. I get worried people are spending more time on their pitches than they are on their actual businesses.

Swayed by urban legends and investor expectations, personal sacrifices are turned into badges of honor. This can hide the truth: Sometimes people simply don't have a good idea, or they're not the right talent to execute it. I once worked with an entrepreneur named Amy for a year. Every time I saw her, she would say something like, "I've been up for three days straight working on my app!"

"Show me what you've built," I'd reply.

Amy never had anything to show me. She was always working on her PowerPoint deck, her model, and any number of other aspects of the app, all without producing a thing. Meanwhile, Amy's app was supposed to be about helping people manage and achieve their goals better and faster.

### IT'S NOT A JOB; IT'S A LIFESTYLE

I personally think being an entrepreneur is a lifestyle. Many people think it's about freedom or being your own boss. But when you're an entrepreneur, you must be committed to learning and growing in everything you do 24/7. You have to know finance. You have to know sales. You have to know marketing. You have to know *everything*. You don't have to be the best at it, but you have to know it. Not knowing is why people fail. When someone pitches me their startup, the first question I ask is about the financials. If they turn it over to their CFO, I get concerned they're not going to make it.

From the lifestyle perspective, being an entrepreneur is about choosing a life where you're constantly working on projects that bring you happiness (and hopefully, making money along the way). Many people tend to forget about the happiness part, focusing instead on the economic win. Instead, being a successful entrepreneur is more like being a successful musician. Imagine if every musician left the business after his or her first song failed to become a hit. That's not how it works. It's about striving to make that second, third, fourth, or fifth song a hit. It's about collaborating with other musicians. Yet, many people tie their commitment to an entrepreneurial life to one project. If the project fails, they quit the whole quest.

Ben is an entrepreneur in Atlanta who left the corporate world to found an e-commerce platform designed to do flash sales with major retailers. Ben did all the right things. He saved a bunch of money over three years and kept his burn rate low. He didn't buy a new house or go on any extra vacations. His plan was great, but it flamed out, because he couldn't find the right partner or compete with places like Amazon and Wal-Mart. Ben shut down his platform and got a corporate job. He's out of the game now forever because he convinced himself this was his one shot. He thought since his company failed, so had he.

What Ben and others like him don't see is the conditions of startup culture inherently create struggle. They blame themselves, thinking they have to work harder and harder. But when you're an entrepreneur, your business is never closed. You can work as much as you want—and, fueled by urban legends, you want to. You believe you have to. That has little to do with reality.

## A NEVER-ENDING STORY

Dabbling in entrepreneurship isn't a real option. Think of it instead as a never-ending story. The sense of free will that comes with being an entrepreneur is unbelievably compelling, and once you get a taste for it, it's tough to go back to a regular job. You can't unring that bell. If that sounds like you, this book was written to help prepare you for the long haul ahead. Everything I'm going to share is rooted in my personal experiences. Founding and running three startups got me hooked on being an entrepreneur, for good and for bad.

I became an entrepreneur for two reasons: necessity and family legacy. The necessity part came from the fact that my dad, Pulla Reddy, had a heart attack when I was fifteen as we were playing tennis one morning. He was around fifty. We were living in India at the time, and there's no 911 in India. After my dad collapsed, I had to get him in the car by myself and race to the hospital. There, he was pronounced dead. From then on, in many ways, I was on my own.

The legacy part comes from the fact that even though my dad was a civil engineer working in a structured environment, he always had an entrepreneurial hustle on the side. My dad taught me it was OK to do things differently. It was OK to ask for more.

My first successful venture happened when I was in college at Georgia Tech. My brother was working for Southern Company (the Southeast's largest utility firm) in a big, corporate office building. I met him for lunch one day, and he introduced me to the company's head of human resources. I was nineteen and didn't even know what HR meant. When I asked the HR chief to explain her job, she said it involved employee wellness and providing perks to keep people happy, so they'd remain at the company. She mentioned the building had a number of good restaurants, and she was looking into providing a dry cleaning service.

"I can do that for you," I replied instantly, even though I knew nothing about dry cleaning.

Everything happened fast. The HR chief gave me free office space to run a dry cleaner out of the building, and I was in business. It was open for two hours in the morning and two hours in the afternoon. At first, I would pick up the dirty clothes in the morning, tag them, and drop them off at a dry cleaning company owned by a friend. He would bring the clean clothes back in the early afternoon, and I would show up a little later and distribute them. Later, I started putting my college buddies to work for me, and all I had to do now was make bank deposits. I was making about $1,200 a month as a college student, and I sold the company after I graduated. I had built something from nothing that could run on its own and keep making me money. Plus, I did it without cash up-front or needing to pay rent. There was no turning back.

### RIDING THE WAVE

My next company was The Reddy Group, a web design company. I started while working at my first real job at the civil engineering firm. I'd charge clients $500 to create a website, then I'd hire my college friends to design it for $250. I was making $5,000 a month on the side—twice as much as I was making as an engineer. Pretty soon, I quit the engineering firm and stole one of their employees (who was also a good friend), and we grew The Reddy Group as partners. We expanded by buying an internet service provider and naming the new venture Cereus Bandwidth. Twelve months later, we were doing $1 million in business and continuing to grow. In the heart of the dot-com boom a couple years later, we merged with another company, went public, and cashed in.

My next venture was Reddy Computer Marketing Services (RCMS), which focused on bringing technology to the construction industry. We were heavily involved in building information modeling (BIM) software, which allows users to design in 3-D in an extremely intelligent way. BIM was revolutionary at a time when everybody was doing drawings in 2-D. We raised a few million, which wasn't hard because, as the CEO, I was judged by investors on the success of Cereus.

## HITTING THE ICEBERG

It took a couple of years for RCMS to find its way, and just when it did, the economy tanked. It was 2008. Every bit of debt we had got called in, and I was given thirty days to come up with it. I had personally guaranteed a huge chunk of that debt.

For the next year, I worked my tail off to keep the company going, constantly spending the night in my office. We were always only one step ahead of disaster and bankruptcy. I was barely able to generate enough business to pay my team and our rent. Investors phoned every day, screaming at me about their losing bet on us. I should have shut down RCMS immediately when things went south, but I refused to give up, believing I, alone, had the superpowers to turn it around. I gained weight, drank too much, and never saw my family. I had been diagnosed with Type 2 diabetes a decade earlier at twenty-eight; my health deteriorated from work and stress.

My then-wife didn't know how much of our finances I'd personally leveraged, and it put a massive strain on our relationship when she found out. We had two young kids and were close to losing our house. She had never understood why I had even started RCMS in the first place, because after my dot-com success, we had more financial security than both of us had ever imagined possible. Before I had jumped into the craziness of the startup world again, she had asked me, "Why can't you just go get a job? Why can't you just be still for a second?"

During this time, I flew up to a conference in Pittsburgh to give a talk about RCMS and the innovation occurring in construction. It was well received, and an audience member who owned a blueprinting business approached me. He didn't realize I was the CEO; he thought I was an RCMS employee and wanted to hire me away to run his digital strategy. To make a long story short, I told him about our near-bankrupt state and how my current responsibility was to try and save the company. He thought we had a great firm stuck in a bad economy and offered to buy us. The deal he outlined was still going to cost me, but it would stop the hemorrhaging and set RCMS on a new course.

## BRUSH WITH DEATH

After negotiating the terms, I flew from Atlanta to San Francisco to close the deal. I took the last flight out on a Sunday evening in early fall. Even though I was exhausted, my start-up frame of mind wouldn't allow me to lean back and sleep, so I set up my laptop and got to work. An hour or so into the flight, I started feeling nauseous. Then I began feeling fidgety, as if I couldn't stay in my seat. I got up to go to the restroom to try and figure out what was going on.

I woke up roughly fifteen minutes later on the floor of the cabin. Three flight attendants hovered over me, trying to make me drink orange juice. One of the attendants had a diabetic son and knew I had crashed because of my condition. When I hadn't come out of the bathroom or responded to repeated knocking, they had broken in, dragged me out, and roused me from unconsciousness.

We landed in San Francisco at 11 p.m. I was shaken up,

worried I might pass out again, but this time without any help. From San Francisco, I still needed to take BART (Bay Area Rapid Transit) to Walnut Creek. It was roughly an hour ride, after which I had to walk from the subway station to my hotel. I tried to think of whom I could call at that moment, but there was no one. I rationalized it was too late in Atlanta to call my wife at the time, that I didn't want to scare her. The truth is, I didn't feel comfortable because our relationship was already so strained. The only person I could think to call was my lawyer, Mike Greenlee. I told Mike what happened, then asked if I could phone him when I reached Walnut Creek and if he would stay on the line with me as I headed to the hotel. If I passed out again, he could call an ambulance.

At midnight, as I walked by myself in the dark to my hotel with my attorney on the other end of the line, the experience of being an entrepreneur who had hit a land mine crystallized something for me. I thought about how when your company is going well, you have lots of people to call when you're in trouble. But when things aren't going well, you don't. You only have the guy you keep on retainer who *has* to take your call. I thought to myself, "What am I doing? If I keep going the way I've been going, my diabetes will get me before anything else. I'm already at the maximum dosage of insulin you can take. I've done all this stuff as an entrepreneur. I've had all this success. So what?"

Start-up culture has a whole meme about failure just being part of the path to success: *Fail fast! Failure is a good thing! Failure is a learning experience!* What gets glossed over are the costs of failing and failing big. I closed the deal in Walnut Creek and made it back to Atlanta without another health crisis. After a few years of commuting to California almost every week, my wife and I got divorced.

## PRETIREMENT

After my divorce, I took a year off—a "pretirement," as I call it. I was determined to be the best dad possible and work on myself. When I was running RCMS, I yelled at employees all the time. Everyone made excuses for my bad behavior, saying I was incredibly smart, but I didn't know how to work with people. The truth is I was always frustrated by the time pressure of trying to make the next deal happen.

During my pretirement, I dropped thirty pounds and went to yoga twice a day. I rented an apartment next to my kids' school and cooked them full-on breakfasts of pancakes, eggs, and bacon. We made forts and obstacle courses with their friends and shot off Nerf guns. In the afternoon, I would come out of the apartment, stand on a hill, and watch my sons as they walked toward me, coming home from school. I'd never done any of that before. I had never been around.

Meanwhile, even though I have a family history of diabetes, I was determined to mitigate the impacts. With diet, meditation, and other measures, I was off insulin in six months and down to a mild dose of meds.

As my pretirement unfolded, I evaluated everything I did to earn money in terms of how it affected my quality of life. People called me to consult, and I turned down every opportunity that would take me away from my commitments to my kids. I also turned down jobs that interrupted my yoga classes and any measure that didn't keep me in good health. I refused to travel or take on huge projects that involved mobilizing a team. I asked potential clients what my time was worth to them. If I didn't agree or the job didn't fit with my schedule, I didn't do it. If the project was boring or the co-workers were jerks, I didn't take it either. My criteria were the work had to be great and so did the people, and I had to add unique value.

Amazingly, when I made my schedule scarce, my price went up. Normally, we think we have to lower our price to work with great clients and on great projects, so we often negotiate ourselves down. We also talk ourselves into working with pain-in-the-ass clients, because the money is good. I, however, experienced the inverse of what most of us believe, working twenty-hour weeks and making more than many people did working eighty.

One day during my pretirement, I created a Venn diagram of myself. The two circles were 1) my skills, and 2) my market. If I focused on the opportunities that fit the intersection of both, I'd always be able to charge a significant amount of money compared to nearly everyone else. If a client is looking for a generic technology consultant, there are a million people to choose from. But if they're looking for a part-time chief technology officer who knows the building industry inside and out, I'm the one to hire because of the scarcity of the pool. Because of that, I could likely charge what I wanted. My goal, I decided, was to focus on work where I was one of the top five people in the world who possessed the needed expertise. As time went on, I realized I was working part-time, making a six-figure income, and providing as much value for clients as when I was working around the clock in startups. With my life in balance, my quality of life drastically improved.

## THE REALITY BEHIND #STARTUPLIFE

When you go on Instagram and type in #startuplife, you see endless photos of tumblers full of whiskey and captions about people fueling themselves with it, because they haven't slept in a week. But false badges of honor keep people trapped in misery. Also, unless you're a lone wolf, and few of us are, your decision to become an entrepreneur will affect countless people around you—especially your significant other, family, and friends. The downward cycle starts with simple things, like cancelling soccer with your best friend. It ends up with situations like my rock bottom: being alone at midnight in a strange city and battling a potentially fatal health crisis with no one to call.

Whether you're starting out as an entrepreneur or are already mid-stream, I hope this book will be a guide and an evergreen reference. Most books about startup life are about the hustle, the grit, and the grind. I want to help entrepreneurs free themselves whenever they feel tempted or trapped by false truths, helping them live meaningful lives across the board instead. The bottom line? I've learned there's no correlation between martyrdom and success.

# PART ONE

# It's OK to Take Care of You

# CHAPTER ONE

# Your Well-Being Is Important

———

*I'll spend time with my kids once I sell.*

*I'll go on vacation once I have an exit.*

*We're going to be next.* (Often said after reading in Tech-Crunch about a company in your sector that just got a big round with a high valuation.)

These are just a few of the myths that drive the entrepreneurial storyline that if you sacrifice hard for three years, you will nab the big win. You'll either sell your company, go public, or receive the next round of funding that will provide the needed resources. It's rarely true. There's always another gate to run through, another hurdle to jump over, and another hill to climb until you can have a life. First, it's series A funding, then B, then C, then the IPO. You tell yourself it will be your turn after you hire a VP of Sales...and then after you hire a new CFO...on and on and on.

The hard truth is once you sign on for the entrepreneurial life, it consumes you. There's a significant chance you'll still be running the company seven years in. You may run it for life. If you exit, you'll probably start another company. If you stay and obtain a big win in the three-year time frame, you'll double down instead of re-evaluating and rebalancing your life. You'll believe you need work twice as hard, otherwise you'll run out of time to take advantage of the opportunity. The entire loop is like being a football player who gets hit hard and ends up with a concussion. What does he want to do after getting the diagnosis? Get right back in the game. Concussions are just part of the sport.

## YOU CAN'T PLAN FOR EVERYTHING

When I started RCMS, I had the grand idea that because I had created a successful startup, sold it within three years, and made a bunch of money, it would automatically happen again. I actually thought it would be easier, since I had investors and my own cash. I didn't account for national and global economic events. I stayed when I should have tried to leave and leave fast. It's common for entrepreneurs to hold on when they should let go.

My friend Jason started a traffic management software company five years ago. We talked the other day, and I asked him to send me his PowerPoint presentation so I could give feedback. He sent it over...and it looked exactly like the one he showed me five years back. "It's taking longer than I thought," Jason said when I asked why. It turns out he's been trying to raise money for the same round of financing and customer acquisition the entire time, putting his real life and his happiness on hold.

The reality is you can be derailed by any number of matters outside of your control, from the stock market to investor woes. There's a huge people factor, too, when it comes to employees. People have babies and go on maternity and paternity leave, they go on vacation, and they have deaths in their families.

Underneath the myth of the three-year exit is the belief entrepreneurs have the ability to control everything, no matter how dark the circumstances. All you have to do is work harder, never let go, never give up. I talk to struggling startup founders all the time who inform me they just hired a new sales guy who is going to save the day.

"He's so great, he could sell ice to Eskimos," I hear.

"He could sell them ice maybe *once*," I reply. "Wouldn't

you rather sell space heaters to Eskimos? Maybe there's something wrong with your product."

## THE NUMBER ONE CAUSE OF STRESS

Entrepreneurs push and push, until they destroy their health, family relationships, and finances. It starts out innocently. You can't make it home for dinner at a decent hour. Over time, that creates a downward spiral that ends up with you missing out or neglecting major life events. When my first son was born, I never changed a single diaper. I thought he didn't need me because a family member who is an entrepreneur told me all newborns do in the first three months is sleep and eat. Since I wasn't doing the breast-feeding, the advice went, I could get a jump on work and take advantage of the fact my son wasn't walking and talking yet. When my second son was born two years later, my then-wife put her foot down. I changed diapers and did much more to help, but I was still always worrying about the next sale and the next investment round. Just because you're physically present for your family, doesn't mean you're actually present.

Meanwhile, good health is dependent on good routines. You would think having lost my dad at fifteen would have made me more conscious of the importance of taking care of myself for my sons. It didn't. In my mind, my startup was the most important thing. The biggest contributor to poor health is stress, and the number one root cause of stress is lying. When we lie to others—and most of all, to ourselves—we create a split in our minds and our bodies. Then we fall into the gap, and the result more often than not is poor health.

A lie can be masked as false optimism, such as telling yourself and your team you're going to raise a large amount of money in the next thirty days. A lie might be you can't afford to eat healthy because you're running a startup. Or that you don't need eight hours of sleep like everyone else; you can't waste all that time. The sleep lie is often rooted in another lie, which occurs when you sell a product knowing it's not ready to go to market...and then you're forced to work around the clock to make it ready. Many entrepreneurs overcommit, because they don't know the difference between being optimistic and unrealistic. Once these lines are blurred, good habits and routines around health and family are left behind, and it's difficult to get them back.

## COLOSSAL FINANCIAL RISKS

Blinded by optimism and brainwashed by urban legends, many entrepreneurs have an inability to accurately assess what's truly happening. This extends to finances. Entrepreneurs continually put it all on the line, risking their homes and their savings. Lenders bank on this risky mindset with loan-marketing strategies, such as letting people eager for startup funding borrow against their IRAs and 401(k)s. Many lenders also play into entrepreneurs' egos. If you show hesitation or discomfort, they say, "If you're not confident about your business, why should we be?"

Let's say you create a startup around a dating app. You go to rent office space in a prime location, and the landlord asks you to document three years' worth of business history and provide your Dun & Bradstreet number. When you reply you're just starting out, he says that's not a problem—all you have to do is personally guarantee the lease instead. You automatically do so because you're certain your app is going to be bigger than Match.com. You're positive the company will crush it. No money is required; all you need to do is sign on the dotted line. The same thing happens when you go to buy office furniture, computers, fixtures, and a foosball table. As you scale up, maybe you borrow more money to cover payroll. That line of credit is keeping you in business. It becomes your primary debt and must be paid off before anything else, especially if investors are involved.

If your startup crashes, bankruptcy isn't far away. I've seen it happen repeatedly. The worst part about a technology company is it has no real assets. Office furniture, computers, foosball tables—it all depreciates to zero. Even though your code may be valuable, no one usually cares about it as a financial asset. In addition, many entrepreneurs invest solely in their own industry, believing they must do so to prove they're all in. That's unfortunately what I did in the dot-com boom. When a bubble bursts, there's nothing inside. That's why they call it a bubble.

## HAPPINESS DENIED

Countless entrepreneurs believe what they do is who they are. The public's fascination with startup culture feeds the phenomenon. If you tell someone at a dinner party you're running your own startup, the response is admiration for your coolness. If you had told them you were an accountant, the response would (maybe) have been polite interest. Entrepreneurs ignore what might make them truly happy—stability, family, and so on—and focus instead on work to bolster the self they show the world.

Phil is an entrepreneur around twenty-nine years old who owned his own web design firm in Atlanta for five years. He's a great guy who attended every startup event in our city, serving on multiple boards of organizations supporting the city's entrepreneur ecosystem and providing volunteer design work. Phil constantly immersed himself in YouTube videos and podcasts on startup culture. One of the last times I saw him, he was clearly stressed out, and I mentioned it must have been from overwork. Phil responded that work was actually slow. I was surprised. Then I was blunt, as I am with people I want to help.

"How much money did you make last year?" I asked him.

Phil wouldn't tell me.

"Show me your tax returns," I insisted. "I'm trying to save you from yourself. How much money did you make?"

"Twenty-eight thousand," he replied.

"Dude, you've been at this for five years," I said. "My interns are making fifteen bucks an hour. Do you want an internship with my company so you can make more money?"

Phil insisted he was simply in a process of building his company, plus his time was caught up in helping our community. I told Phil the most beneficial thing he could do for our community would be to help himself. I gave him a lead on an excellent job at a startup organization paying $125,000 a year. The hiring manager loved Phil and offered him the position on the spot. He turned it down. When I urged Phil to reconsider, advising that he could still run his web design firm on the side, Phil still refused.

"The community will view me as a sellout," he said. "Besides, I think I can make my company work."

Phil has since moved to Silicon Valley, believing that a new location would solve the problem of his flagging sales and tiny income. My bet: $28K isn't going to go far in the Bay Area. Like so many others, Phil is too attached to making sure his persona in both the world and the digital world (LinkedIn, Facebook, Instagram) stays "entrepreneur." By doing so, his financial and personal stability is put on the back burner while his stress is on the front.

## HOT STOVES

Even when founders burn out and their startups implode, they can't help themselves from jumping back into the game. They might take time off for a little while, recharge, refresh, and mull becoming a schoolteacher. Then, they hop back on the wheel. The reason is most entrepreneurs don't define happiness for themselves; they define it instead by what they see around them in the startup media world. They believe the path to personal and professional fulfillment is in becoming a successful startup entrepreneur, then an angel investor, and finally, a venture capitalist.

Failure breeds success as long as you *learn* from your failures. I'm not certain entrepreneurs today are learning from their failures and doing things differently when they re-enter the startup world. It doesn't seem to matter that they've touched the hot stove of entrepreneurship and gotten burned working 24/7. They've felt miserable, gone bankrupt, and lost important relationships. But they can't stay away.

Today, countless entrepreneurs dream of being a Chris Sacca or a Dave McClure instead of a Bill Gates, whose mission was first and foremost to build a great company and employee culture over the long haul. I hear entrepreneurs talk all the time about how many people they've hired or which heavy hitter they've brought on, instead of how they're changing the lives of their customers. These entrepreneurs aren't motivated to start a company to solve a big problem. To be fair, many founders start out with a vision for creating change, but that vision inevitably shifts when outside investors enter the picture. As a result, fundraising and hiring often become tools for personal validation, and then they've lost their way.

## PUSH, PUSH, PUSH

When a failed entrepreneur jumps back into startup land without changing what didn't work—or examining his or her role in a failed venture—they're like CrossFitters who work out until they need new knees, yet go back to the same punishing regime after surgery. They're like people who go on every crash diet, but then gain all the weight back when they stop because nothing's changed in how they manage stress and their lives. They believe in the saying: "If a car runs out of gas, you keep pushing the pedal." Try that on the freeway and see how it works.

The reality is extremes don't work. If you're sick, you should rest or go to the doctor. If you don't want to get out of bed for whatever reason, you probably shouldn't. If your loved ones are feeling neglected, they need your time.

If you let your startup overtake your life, it burns everything in its path. If you're the person at the top and you're not leading a balanced, healthy existence, it affects everyone and everything else around you. Leading a company requires a great deal of personal energy. Recharging isn't a luxury, but a necessity.

One of my most recent companies, Softwear Automation, is a robotics business we spun out of Georgia Tech. We created robots that made apparel. I was determined to do things differently than I'd done in the past. We recruited great people, and I told them I wanted them to be productive for thirty hours a week. The other ten should be spent either thinking critically about their lives or screwing around.

"If I see you here on the weekend," I told my staff, "we're going to have a conversation. Either you've underestimated your workload, or I need to help you with more resources or training."

With ground rules and a mission, the company thrived during my tenure. *The Wall Street Journal*, *The Economist*, and other media outlets wrote we were revolutionizing the apparel industry. But we ignored the buzz and just focused on what was working and what wasn't. When I realized figuring out how to get robots to make jeans and T-shirts was much harder than I envisioned, I decided to focus on flat items like rugs and towels. We recognized we had finite time and resources, and we succeeded because we worked within our limitations. By contrast, numerous startups act like they have infinite time and resources. When a huge challenge appears, founders tell employees, "Figure it out. Just figure it out." The result: Everyone's nights and weekends are swallowed up by work.

At the robotics company, I celebrated the small wins. In the past, a $10,000 deal would have meant little to me. I would have told my employees, "We can do better." Instead, I created optimism around the small wins, because I had learned they lead to bigger ones, and those lead to massive wins.

## A NEW PARADIGM

What I discovered during and after my pretirement is that when your life is in balance, you operate in peak performance mode. Energy is high; thinking is clear. You're not overextending yourself physically, emotionally, and financially. When you create limitations around what you choose to do and for how long, you prioritize more efficiently. You see projects executed from beginning to end, and that is extremely satisfying. Unfocused, work-crazed entrepreneurs end up with countless half-baked cakes, sinking a great deal of time, effort, and money into multiple directives with zero results.

Finally, when you get into balance, your bank account will reflect it. If you're making $100,000 at a startup while working four thousand hours a year, that's different from making the same salary while working two thousand. When you fit work around your life instead of life around your work, everything shifts for the better. Try it and see for yourself.

# CHAPTER TWO

# Be Well-Rounded

---

"It's about the culture!" I hear this again and again. Culture is one of the most talked about words among startups, but has anyone truly looked at the word? Specifically, at the root of the word?

The root of *culture* is *cult*. As nearly everyone knows, cults normally don't end well. Usually, the leader ends up getting shot in the backyard of a compound by the FBI, or something like that. Cults typically aren't successful because they aren't built to survive. When startup founders start rhapsodizing to me about their culture, my response is to suggest they proceed with a little caution. A startup's culture can unknowingly drive negative behavior and negative expectations.

One of the key characteristics of a cult is you're asked (or required) to set aside your personal interests and opinions for those of the group. You're no longer allowed to have an independent thought or position. Cults demand its members make sacrifices to belong. In religious and spiritual cults, that can be your worldly possessions. In the startup world, it's your time—working late nights, working through weekends, working so much you don't have a personal life or even remember what one is. There's a fine line between having a positive and productive culture and a cult mentality.

Many investors unfortunately treat entrepreneurship like indentured servitude. They believe if you take a reasonable salary as an entrepreneur, it means you're not committed. At RCMS, I didn't take a salary for almost four years because that's what investors expected. I didn't even see anything wrong with it. *Work eighty hours a week. Don't think about getting paid. Focus on the upside.* These are the things being an entrepreneur has come to mean—not focusing on your well-being, your livelihood, or your family.

A VC said to me the other day, "I want entrepreneurs who are living lean and eating ramen noodles."

My response, "Why would anybody of great capability do that when they have countless opportunities outside of this startup?"

When I coach entrepreneurs, I suggest they change their

vocabulary and call their company a "project" instead. If you're doing a writing project, you're not usually thinking, *I'm going to give up my family and all of my other interests for the rest of my life and kill myself over this one project.* A project has a beginning and an end. When it's done, hopefully you've made some money and done some work you're proud of.

Investors don't like to hear me espouse views like that. I had one ask me if I was trying to unionize entrepreneurs. But it's critical for entrepreneurs to know there's no need to believe extreme sacrifice must be part of the equation. The focus should be on whether you can provide an interesting solution to a problem and how you're going to execute that idea—not about whether you fit in to a cult.

An investor asked me recently, "If an entrepreneur wants to come work for me and get paid $30,000 a year, why is that your business?"

My response was, "It's just bad for the ecosystem and the community."

I worry people will look back on the decades they spent working nonstop and think: *What did I really accomplish? Why did I sacrifice so much?* It might end up being akin to how people once thought razing forests was a good thing because there were plenty of trees to go around. Well, there aren't so many trees anymore—and trees prevent landslides when the rains come through.

## PERSONAL INTERESTS FOSTER BALANCE

Most entrepreneurs wind up putting their personal interests on hold; they become single-focused, thinking the harder they work at one thing, the more successful they'll be. What I've experienced is leading a well-rounded life will make you better at everything you pursue—*especially* your business. Everything in your life is connected, just as it is in your body. If you want to lift a heavy object, you don't use just your wrist or your hand or your bicep. Go try to lift something heavy with just your wrist. It's not just hard—it's impossible. Lifting heavy stuff requires different muscle groups throughout your body working in concert.

Personal interests that lead to balance can be anything from messing around with a bass guitar and painting to having a blast with your kids, getting enough exercise, eating well, and playing sports. (By playing sports you get the added benefit of learning how to help your co-workers thrive. I've insisted my kids each choose a team sport to play for this reason. They've learned that when people let you down, you still have to stay positive and play the rest of the game together. You don't yell at them. You put your arm on their shoulder and look ahead at the next opportunity.)

## IT'S ABOUT ART, NOT SUCCESS

When RCMS was bought, my new office was located in the basement of one of Atlanta's old-school print shops. No windows. No roof garden. I hit it off immediately with the graphic designer, Buffy. Everyone else was suit-and-tie. I was the guy in a T-shirt and jeans, and Buffy had the hippie, artist vibe.

Buffy was incredibly talented and had been there forever. When I asked her why she hadn't moved on, she told me about the two bands she had been playing in for years and about how she was also a painter and sculptor. I still didn't get it. I asked her why she was still in the bands if they hadn't "made it." "I'm an artist. It's not about success. It's about doing art," she said. Making logos was her day job, and that was fine with her. But everything Buffy did for work was amazing even if it was just a flyer for a chicken wing shop. Her outside creativity wound up informing all her work.

I admitted to Buffy that I would goof around with the guitar, but I never got anywhere. From her I eventually learned it's not about trying to get a record deal, and I didn't have to be a professional artist to do good art. I could paint and sketch and jam for my own enjoyment. It all mattered. Plenty of studies exist that show how learning an instrument, exercising, and working with your hands can make you less stressed and improve brain efficiency. That proved to be the case for me.

Perhaps more importantly, creativity helped change my analytical mind. It transformed the way I engage with people. Too often, work defines who we are. Think how often someone asks you, "What do you do for a living?" I used to ask that all the time. Now I ask, "What are you into?" I might even go so far as to ask people, "What kind of trouble have you gotten into lately?" If you aren't getting into trouble, you aren't having fun. You always need to be stirring up a little trouble here and there. (Some of the most seemingly straight-laced old men give the best responses. "Not nearly enough," they say. "What did you have in mind?")

Artistic activities helped me shift my focus that work isn't just about business and numbers. It's about relationships. In a world of conference calls, it might not always be efficient for two new colleagues to drive forty minutes each to meet for a cup of coffee, but it is a much better way to build a relationship. I use work applications like Slack, but it kills me when I see two people sitting next to each other communicating with them. Personal connections are not created that way. You need the subtleties of face-to-face communications. There are many weeks where I could have a remote meeting, but instead I bring coffee and breakfast to my colleagues, and we talk over ideas with no agenda.

Today, we live in a world with constant feedback loops.

We've come to expect fast or automatic responses, and relationships aren't forged in a text exchange. Artistic activities promote deeper relationships because they teach you how to slow down. Relationships aren't about being productive and hitting metrics but about being real.

## THE POWER OF EXPLORATION

We also live in a society now where convenience is everywhere, so of course we should take advantage of it. But if a robot is cleaning our floors, and we're driving less because we're using Lyft, and we're using efficiency apps all day long, then...what exactly are we going to do with all the extra time? My worry is we will find ways to cure our boredom that won't always be the healthiest. As the saying goes: boredom is the devil's playground.

We might drink more, for example. "Let's grab a drink," is a normal part of our vocabulary, as opposed to, "Hey, let's go for a walk," or, "Let's go take a pottery class."

One solution to the time surplus is to use it for exploration. I've decided to try to learn something new every year. This year, it's welding. I have no reason other than I think the masks and sparks are cool, and I'm interested in what parts of my brain I can activate. It might be a different pursuit for you. Whether it's welding, painting, playing guitar, or riding your bike, all those things will prevent many of us from finding ourselves staring at the bottom of a martini glass when 6:15 p.m. rolls around because we aren't sure what else to do. I wouldn't count out nonsense activities either, like adult coloring books. There's a reason they're flying off the shelves. My girlfriend, Rachel, and I travel quite a bit. We were recently in Estonia. I went for a hike, and she found me in the woods using my civil engineering background to build fairy houses out of twigs. I didn't post any of the structures on Instagram because it wasn't about accomplishment; it was about play. Taking the time to play like children is a great release and also a great team-building exercise.

## SYNCHRONICITY

Not having a "plan" leaves us space to pick our heads up and have actual experiences. When you're engaged in exploration, synchronicity often mysteriously follows. When Rachel and I were exploring a town in Estonia, a large black bear crossed our path. That evening, I spoke at an event, and when I mentioned the bear to a group of people at the party afterward, they were flabbergasted. Most of them didn't believe me at first. In the entire region, they said, there are only about ten black bears.

A similar experience happened to us in Asheville, North Carolina. We were driving around with no agenda when we saw cars and people with binoculars lined up on the

e of the road. We pulled over. People told us they'd
en camping for days in order to see the monarch but-
erflies migrating down to Mexico. No one knew when
the butterflies would show up. As we stood there, they
did. These types of experiences keep happening to me
the more I let myself play and explore. If I travel with an
agenda, I'm not as open to possibility, and I miss out on
more experiences than I gain. Living like an artist con-
nects you to greater forces.

Many of us get sucked into the idea of time management, so we read multiple blogs, check off tasks, and
make Trello boards. But when you have wants and pas-
sions outside of work, you naturally prioritize your work
around what's truly important. As of this writing, I am
involved with twelve companies as a founder, investor, or
advisor. "There's no way you can be this Zen with twelve
companies," I'm told all the time. "You have to be more
stressed out." The reason I'm not is because I hire the right
employees and delegate responsibly, which allows me to
focus on what's important. Agile software development
methodologies where you work in two-week sprints are
the rage today, and that can be effective for short-term
projects. But building a business is a long-haul effort if
you're doing it right. You won't last if you're trying to
run a marathon a day. Don't get caught up in how many
hours you're clocking. Focus on what helps you flourish.
Take care of yourself first, and let yourself be surprised

at the results. Later in this book, I write about my theory of Natural Harmonics. It also plays an important role.

## LISTEN TO YOUR BODY

It's difficult to slow down because startup culture is fueled by a go-go-go mentality that tells us to keep pushing. It's created an epidemic of people who don't pay attention to how they're feeling. Becoming highly balanced requires you to listen to your body. It will tell you everything you need to know but only if you take the time to listen.

### LISTEN WHEN YOU'RE TIRED

For decades, I had insomnia. I worked three jobs in college, and while running my first startup, I had the brilliant idea I would sleep better if I had a couple drinks before bed. After college, while working full-time with a startup on the side, I bought into the idea I didn't need as much sleep as most people. I used to tell them I'd calibrated my body to need only five hours a night. I was special, superhuman-like.

Today, I try hard to get a minimum of eight hours of sleep a night, and sometimes ten. This shocks people. They think it must be impossible for me to get anything accomplished. It's assumed there's a correlation between how little sleep you're getting and how hard you're working.

This is nonsense. I formed my new sleep habits during pretirement. Since I didn't have to be anywhere, I didn't set my alarm. My body fell into its natural rhythm, and I was continually refreshed and recharged. I hadn't felt that way in years. Whenever I'd take on a consulting project, I'd crank it out with energy to spare and wonder what I was going to do for the rest of the day.

We wake up every morning, and we have free will for maybe five seconds. Stop, breathe, and think for ten seconds that free will is the one superpower that most of us have. After that, kids' schedules, work, significant others, taxes, and other priorities take over. Free will is vaporized. Exhaustion often follows. When you get enough sleep, you're able to work optimally on all levels. During pretirement, I was left to do only what I wanted. I became skillful at assessing my time, separating the *shoulds* from the *wants*. It's nearly impossible to get this kind of clarity without enough sleep.

### LISTEN WHEN YOU'RE HUNGRY

Meanwhile, we all know when we're hungry. It's primal. But the startup way is to eat junk because it's convenient. There's no time for nourishment. When it comes to food, I believe we should either eat for the body or eat for the soul. As long as it fits into one of those two categories, it simplifies what I buy or order off a menu. You might have a kale smoothie because that's what your body needs. If you want to eat cheesecake though, eat the best cheesecake you can find to feed your soul, not the diet cheesecake.

You can't eat food for the body all the time or food for the soul all the time and expect to find balance. Fullness isn't always satisfaction. Satisfaction is about being nourished by a great eating experience. I'm a big fan of portion control, so I might order a killer cheesecake in New York, but then eat half. That's a challenge because I grew up in a family where if I didn't clean my plate, my parents lectured me about starving kids in Africa. Today, I don't make it a goal to finish everything in front of me.

## YOUR BODY IS THE SMARTEST DEVICE YOU HAVE

When I returned to India recently, and my extended family asked me, "Are you reverse aging? Are you going to the gym? You look great; what's going on with you?" They were in disbelief when I said I was doing yoga, gentle walks, and a little hiking. I don't believe in beating the snot out of my body at the gym. I'm not trying to kill myself or hurt my knees. I'm not impressed with being sore after a twenty-mile run. That sounds horrible—why would you do that to yourself?

Intense workout classes are ubiquitous, and the goal when you take them is to "crush it." To get great exercise, though, all you need to do is go outside and walk. No apps, methods, or special skills required. I've heard people say, "I should start walking more. I'm going to go buy some new shoes and a Fitbit." What? No, just go walk! Too many of us think technology knows us better than we know ourselves. That mindset starts early. I was once invited to Google's Atlanta campus to speak to a bunch of high school students. The program was designed to educate inner city kids about entrepreneurship. Most of the attendees were around fifteen to eighteen years old. One asked me, "Hey, what do you think about Fitbits and all of these devices?"

"You're born with the smartest device you'll ever have," I said. "Your body. All you have to do is hone in and learn to listen to it instead of ignoring it."

One hundred kids and a bunch of their parents stared back at me; many looked confused. I was in one of the most tech-obsessed places in the universe, yet I was dispensing the advice that smart devices are stupid. While Fitbits and Jawbones can give you a lot of information, you don't need them when you're in tune with yourself. Again, your body will tell you everything you need to know. Besides, if you aren't listening to your body, you might not listen to a fitness tracker, either. Perhaps that's why Jawbone went out of business. I recently was given an Apple Watch. I thought I wouldn't use it. Three months later and after a week of hiking in Slovenia, I loved it. A few weeks after that, I was going through security in LaGuardia, and I lost it. I went a week without the watch and ended up buying another one. Why? The "breathe" app. I'm less interested in how many steps I have, but having my day interrupted and being told to breathe has been priceless.

## CREATE YOUR OWN LIFE

Ultimately, the way to find balance is to figure out what's a priority and what's not. It's not uncommon for the people I work with to accuse me of being lax on responding to email.

"You never asked me a question," I respond.

I'm a helpful person, but you have to ask. I read every email, but not every one requires a response. Everyone talks about work/life balance, but you can't force yourself to create it the way people force themselves to do CrossFit squats. You have to want to create balance in part because there are other things you prefer to be doing. During my pretirement, I learned your real job is to be an artist whose greatest creation is your own life. When you're an artist, you think for yourself. By doing that, you're less likely to follow cults, and when you tap into what's unique to you, life flows. About once a quarter, I file for email bankruptcy. I take all my unread emails and delete them (at this moment I have 1,884). If it is important, I will come back. Last time I checked, I was not in the email business; I'm in the people business.

# CHAPTER THREE

# Value Your Own Time

——

The typical employee reaction to being overstressed or overworked is to find another job. The typical entrepreneur's reaction to being overstressed or overworked is to work harder. He or she can't just go find another job. There are no bosses to blame, no corporations calling the shots. So they start doing what my girlfriend, Rachel, calls "entrepreneur math." That's when there are twenty-four hours in a workday, not eight.

Another kind of entrepreneur math comes into play when people don't qualify their investors and customers. I'm often copied on emails about a fantastic meeting a startup founder had with a big fish. I just met with Coca-Cola, and they're very interested! However, when I ask how much money the potential investor is willing to put in, the answer is, "Nothing yet, but he or she 'loves' the company." Unfortunately, emotional optimism can make entrepreneurs feel like they have traction when they don't. They're driven by possibility and work harder and harder to execute an idea when no outside commitment exists. Entrepreneurs then run the risk of living inside a fictional universe of accomplishment. There's a difference between opportunity and money in the bank.

As a result of all this, entrepreneur math feeds a CrossFit approach to startup life. People sweat and grunt and tear up their muscles, working themselves to misery before getting a little rest and starting all over again. The "work harder" mindset has entrepreneurs mistakenly believing they have infinite time and opportunity. (If a corporation required them to work this hard, they'd push back, saying it was unreasonable if not impossible.)

As a group, entrepreneurs also tend to be highly reactive; they're pulled in countless directions. They live off—and get obsessed with—the optimism of the "next," meaning the next idea, change or challenge, the next client and investor. Prioritization goes out the window; instead, they work through weekends chasing every opportunity. The truth is, for reactive types, an overflow of unfiltered opportunities is not optimal. A typical first-time startup entrepreneur will send an email blast out about his new product and be thrilled when a hundred people respond and say they're interested in finding out more. The entrepreneur makes a plan to call every single one. But depending on the "ask" in the email, not a single prospect may buy or invest in the product. When you're only one person, having a hundred opportunities is not necessarily a good problem. I've found it's better to focus on a small number of high-quality prospects instead of multiple ones that might be a bad fit. I also focus on prospects that frustrate me, ones for whom I know one of my products could be a game changer. Conventional advice is to not waste time if people don't respond. But I can't do that. My philosophy is: "Let me help you be more successful."

## AFRAID OF A "NO"

In my experience, there's zero correlation between the amount of work you put in and the success of your startup. In fact, if you're serving a true need, and you have a great product, you shouldn't have to work so hard. If you are, something might be wrong.

Craig and Mark were twentysomethings building an app designed to be a LinkedIn for job-hunting college students. One night, I came out of a restaurant and handed my ticket to the valet. I looked up and realized it was Craig. He told me he worked all day on the startup but needed to park cars at night to pay the bills. He and Mark ultimately never made anything happen with their company. They could walk into a room of potential investors and describe their product with skill and unlimited enthusiasm. What they couldn't do was directly ask one of the investors present if he or she would put in $100,000. Like so many new entrepreneurs, they were afraid of hearing a *no* because then the wind might get knocked out of their sails. The other common reaction to a *no* is to become defensive, blaming investors who "don't get it." Both reactions can be overcome by understanding that often the right answer to a request for funds contains a *yes* and a *no*: interest plus hesitation. With that response, it's your job then to convince an investor of your company's or product's value and close a deal. Craig and Mark fell into the trap of using the work-harder mindset to avoid telling the truth to themselves. But truth-telling filters out weak opportunities.

## HOW TO VALUE YOUR TIME

Many entrepreneurs forget how valuable their time is. They like to tell people they're "the CEO and chief bottle washer" of their companies. If you're answering phones because you don't have anyone else to do it, that's one thing. But if you're answering phones because your attention is too scattered, that's another. My advice, again, is to focus on high-value tasks. When an investor calls on a Saturday, and you're on the soccer field with your kids, try letting it go to voicemail. If the voicemail says it's urgent, of course you return the call. If it's not, do you need to?

I try and drop the attitude that everything needs to get done yesterday and separate the myth from the reality of what is best for me and my companies. The myth of doing more hard work is seductive, but committing to valuing your time saves you pain and heartbreak down the road. Aligning your resources with a real opportunity is the best way to go.

I mentor two entrepreneurs who work at their startups while taking consulting gigs on the side to ease the financial pressure. They each work forty hours a week: twenty consulting at one hundred dollars an hour and twenty at their own companies. Both entrepreneurs tell me if they were working forty hours a week solely on their startups, they'd be progressing at the same rate but with less cash flow and more stress on their personal lives. When you flip the paradigm, focusing on your well-being instead of what your investors want, you're more likely to be successful. Sacrifice at all costs isn't workable for the long term.

## 'THIS WILL NEVER END'

It was Christmas Break, 1999. I was with my family at my brother's house having a great time celebrating the holiday. Then my cell rang. My company had recently gone public in the heart of the dot-com boom, and it was our new CEO telling me I needed to jump on a plane to New York to sign a sales contract. If I didn't, the sale wouldn't be counted for the year-end quarter, which would not make the investors happy. It was a pre-DocuSign era.

During the flight, I thought to myself, "What am I doing? I could have sold the company, paid off what I owed, stayed home for Christmas, and sat on my butt for five years instead of being on this plane." I flew into LaGuardia and took a taxi across the deserted streets to Midtown. Coming from Atlanta, I felt like a country mouse in that cab because I had been to New York only once before, also for work, but had traversed it via a company Town Car.

My family was disappointed when I'd had to leave Christmas dinner, but they were also supportive. I was a high-status person now who had to do what needed to be done for success—in this case, ink a multimillion-dollar deal. But in that cab, a part of me realized I was being driven by imposter syndrome. I was worried I didn't know what I was doing now as a top executive of a publicly held company, so I better act like I did. I wanted to prove I wasn't a small-fry entrepreneur who had gotten lucky. That's when I realized the current trip wasn't going to be an anomaly. I was likely going to be pulled away from my life and my loved ones for countless times in the foreseeable future. "This will never end," I thought to myself. For years, it didn't. Vacations were never vacations, and I was never off during off-hours.

## STOP, PAUSE, BREATHE, THINK

During my pretirement, I learned when your life is in a state of balance, a deep level of clarity follows. That allows you to do things that far exceed any accomplishments made in a state of exhaustion. To achieve this state, you have to develop the ability to stop, pause, breathe, and think. That lets you assess how much time is required for any project and how to execute it as best and efficiently as possible. When a large software company asked me to take on a complex marketing project for one of their new products, it took me three days during my pretirement. It had taken me four weeks to accomplish a similar task in my previous life because of burnout. Because I was in balance during pretirement, the project wasn't grueling. It didn't even feel like work—every aspect flowed, from the writing to the research. I still took walks, met friends, and went to yoga and kickboxing. I carpooled, spent time with my kids, and got everyone's laundry done. In the past, I had always fit my life around my work. Now, I was fitting my work around my life.

The urban legend of startup land is the more time you spend working, the more money you'll make. But if you spend four hours at the gym instead of one, are you going to be four times bigger and four times stronger? Probably not. The solution is to guard your time. You only have so much of it. I've learned to guard my space, energy, and time by simply asking, "Why?"

For example: *Why should I respond to this email?* I rarely respond to emails that don't have a specific "ask."

*Why specifically do I need to be in this meeting or on this conference call? What is my role?* "I'm the CEO," isn't a good enough answer. If I'm just there as window dressing, I can introduce myself and go mute when the meeting or call starts. Or if you want me to be at a ballgame with clients, I can do it, but don't ask me to be there without clarifying the role I'm expected to play. I want to be highly available to customers and my team, but being highly available requires a *reason*.

When you exert free will, you remember who you are and what you want. Otherwise, you're a zombie. Whenever possible, I suggest offloading, hiring, or delegating tasks you're not thrilled about doing to others who are. When I bring a new salesperson in to one of my companies, I train and prepare them extensively. When they're good to go, I arrange for us to meet their first prospect together...but then I'll call ten minutes beforehand and say I'm occupied: they're flying solo. The salespeople always excel because they've been well trained. If I accompany them the first time, there's an expectation for me to be present in every meeting and on every call. Instead, by kicking them out of the nest, even when they might not believe they're ready, I create freedom for myself.

## THE THEORY OF NATURAL HARMONICS

Another way to avoid wasting time is to understand the theory of natural harmonics. Pouring twice as much water on a plant doesn't make it grow twice as fast. Certain activities progress at their own pace, and neither you nor outside forces can meaningfully accelerate them. Most entrepreneurs struggle with following the rhythm of natural harmonics (myself included; I'm still learning). But believing we can overcome natural harmonics is like believing we can influence world events, the weather, or even the personal vibes of our employees. We can't control everything. This is also why I work on so many projects; I push hard on the ones with little friction. When it comes to projects that are immovable, I give them time or eventually shut them down. Failed projects are common. Things get highly personalized when you only have one project and you have nothing else to work on.

Many entrepreneurs come from flawed corporate environments where work moved as slow as molasses, and they're bursting with ideas and itching to overhaul old processes. When they leave these big, unwieldy companies and go at it alone, the pendulum swings the other way. When things don't happen as quickly as they thought, they get frustrated and work harder, which isn't the answer. No matter how many sales calls you make, clients will usually get back to you on their own schedules. Believing you can find, thoroughly interview, and hire a top-level person in only two weeks is fiction.

You can neither know for certain what will work with your company nor foresee what will go viral, no matter how much your research and modeling predicts hockey-stick growth. In fact, the ubiquitous claims by entrepreneurs of hockey-stick growth are nearly all fiction. People have exhaustively studied why Facebook became huge, but do we really know why? Almost two decades ago, online grocery business Webvan raised $800 million, but the business only lasted for a few years before it went bankrupt. It was seen as a huge failure—the poster child of dot-com era excess. Webvan was bought by Amazon, which fashioned AmazonFresh from its DNA and successfully launched the online grocery delivery company in 2007. Online grocery delivery was never a bad idea, but the world wasn't ready for Webvan when it came out. It wasn't the right time.

Jimmy is an entrepreneur I know who worked for four years on an app where you can pay your restaurant bill yourself if you don't want to wait for the server to bring it to you. He made the rounds, but no one was interested; they were already working with one of Jimmy's competitors. Jimmy eventually ran out of most of his capital. He battened down the hatches, reduced staff to a skeleton team to stay afloat, and held on. When his competitor announced it was going into the cash register business to compete with the likes of Clover and Square, many people in the point-of-sale world weren't interested in that route. All of a sudden, Jimmy was in business.

## NATURAL HARMONICS AND PERSONAL EFFICIENCY

Rather than pushing harder when things don't happen, listening to yourself and others is the answer. If an entrepreneur pitches forty investors without getting any funding, maybe he or she should rethink the business model, whether they are the right person to run the business, and whether the timing is right.

Experience has taught me practical timing issues. For example, never pitch your startup to investors in October. Most investors are wealthy, and rich folks go on vacation for Thanksgiving, to Turks and Caicos for Christmas, and to Europe for the time period around New Year's Eve. They aren't in a hurry to write a check until January or February. Instead, from Thanksgiving until January, focus on improving your product, acquiring new customers, and spending time with your family. Meanwhile, one the worst things you can do for your quality of life is have your year-end quarter line up with the end of a calendar year. That's what put me on that plane to New York on Christmas Eve.

Following natural harmonics reduces the time you wait

around, creates realistic expectations, reduces stress, and enhances personal productivity. It also leads to employees and companies finding a rhythm that works for them. Because startup culture normally has everyone working seven days a week, breaks are important to avoid hitting the plateau that inevitably comes from constantly being in reactive mode. A business has a metabolism. You can't go around ruining it and expect the business to stay healthy.

While numerous companies have work-from-home policies on Fridays and even Mondays, I found work-from-home Wednesday is best for my teams. Working remotely on Friday often results in people taking a three-day weekend, while working remotely on Monday creates problems because face time is often needed with colleagues. On Wednesdays, everyone in my company seems to crank out work that doesn't require collaboration.

Companies go back and forth between open office environments and closed ones, between allowing people to work remotely to insisting on an in-office presence. All the options are valuable because every person operates differently. Some people can't work from home. Period. Others work best from their laptops at the breakfast table while still in pajamas. An employee at one of my companies wasn't required to work in the office, but his social makeup was such that he needed to connect with others daily. He commuted to the office every day because he understood that in order to give his best, the synergy of others was essential. My best advice is to scrap policies and guidelines and instead show up when you're at your best and give everyone else permission to do the same.

# PART TWO

# *Be All About People*

# CHAPTER FOUR

# Take Care of Others to Take Care of Yourself

Locker-room culture is such that if you put a group of guys in a room, many believe they can make degrading comments about women. A misogynistic, Wild West attitude pervades startups in particular. We've seen it happen at places like Uber, where female employees were reportedly propositioned for sex by male superiors; when they told Human Resources, nothing was done. We've seen it with people like entrepreneur and angel investor Dave McClure, who admitted to similar behavior after a New York Times story reported on it (McClure's Twitter confession: "I'm a creep.").

When it comes to startups, how did the "no handbook, no

HR, no problem" urban legend get started? People who've worked at big corporations are used to being constrained by a fear of getting in trouble with HR. As a result, when they arrive at startups, many think they don't have to give a shit about rules. In addition, numerous startup founders who put "CEO" on a business card for the first time suddenly think they can behave differently. That mentality glosses over the fact that as a leader, you do need to build the right environment. You do need to set clear standards for what's OK and what's not. But an employee handbook alone can't be the only guardrail for a startup's behavior.

My company, startup incubator The Combine, doesn't have a printed handbook, but that doesn't mean we don't have a culture or rules. It's not a free-for-all. Everybody knows the rules, and we constantly discuss how we need to treat each other. Multiple conversations take place throughout the recruiting process about what behavior is good for us, the business, and investors. We prioritize treating people well and working well together. We're not the best teaching organization, I often say, but we're a very good learning organization. We might lack the structure of training programs, but there's a great deal of on-the-job learning. It's not a great fit for everyone. If it's not a fit, it doesn't make them a bad employee, and it doesn't make me a bad employer (former employees could disagree with the latter). It just wasn't a fit.

For example, you don't need a sick day policy to know how to treat people when they get sick. When one of my employees comes down with a stomach virus, my first question isn't, "Who's covering your work?" It's not important. What's important is how they're feeling and whether they need anything. No company is going out of business if someone gets ill. Life will happen, and as a leader you have to factor that into the workflow. I didn't always operate this way. At RCMS, I fostered a "suck it up" mentality. Take a Tylenol and get back to work. I would get annoyed when someone got the flu.

"This is a people business," founders will often say about their companies. But everything is a people business. The relationships and the interactions you have with your people are all you have. If you're a larger organization, it's not realistic to communicate to every employee, but leaders set the tone and how that tone is embedded in the company every day. Founders also often say they don't need an org chart. "We're flat," they pronounce. But you do need to manage people and manage them well. It's possible to do so without being dictatorial. One way to accomplish that is to understand what team members are great at, what they do, and what they don't want to do. When it comes to the latter, a cooperative recognition of what needs to happen is key: "Hey, I know you don't want to do this, but we need to. I'm open to different ways to get it done if you have any ideas." That's different than saying, "Go get it done, period."

## POWER-TRIPPING

Startup founders have to be careful not to succumb to power trips. When I was running RCMS, I sent an employee I'll call Steve to India to visit a company performing software programming for us. Steve's trip took place during the time period when RCMS was sinking. We were two months behind on payroll; the pressure was excruciating. I sent Steve over because we thought our vendor might be lying about how many people were working on our project and their skill levels. On his first day at their office, Steve figured out we were right about the monkey business. The vendor realized Steve was on to them and kicked him out, telling Steve the company wouldn't work with us anymore until it was paid in full.

Steve had never been to India. He wasn't the world traveler type. Back at his hotel, he called me and asked what he should do.

"Fuck them," I said. "We'll find someone else."

Steve reminded me the vendor still had a key piece of RCMS hardware.

"You need to fucking go get it," I responded.

Steve was stunned. "What do you mean go get it? How do I do that? I don't even know where their office is located. I was there once."

"I pay you good money to solve problems," I said. "Just make it happen. I don't care what you have to do. If you want to come back, you're going to have to buy your own ticket, or you better get used to living there. And tell your wife you're not coming back."

Steve was never able to obtain our hardware. In spite of my threats, his ticket had already been paid for, and it was round-trip. He flew home. I laid him off two weeks later, not because of the India incident but because we couldn't afford to pay him anymore.

Would I behave that way today? Absolutely not. I don't tell employees that if I say jump, they have to ask: How high? People don't join startups to be treated that way. They don't want to work for jerks, and founders who treat people poorly often find themselves abandoned by the very employees they need to succeed. Good people can always find another job. Only those who are less in demand and are less capable will stick around, and they probably can't help founders get where they want to go. Nearly every study about why employees are happy at work reports it's rarely about money. It's about the work environment and quality of life. A power-tripping, pain-in-the-ass boss is not high on the list of what any of us want.

## EVOLUTIONARY VS. REVOLUTIONARY

Earlier, I said a founder can manage people without being dictatorial, aka "the boss." In order to do so, it's important to recognize startups are ultimately about troubleshooting problems to create processes that will scale. Corporations, on the other hand, are about improving an existing process. I like to use the analogy of buildings. In the startup mindset, you're building the factory and the machines, and making sure things work efficiently so the business can get up and running. Corporations are more about running the building—making sure expenses are down, the space is taken care of, and the janitors are taking out the trash.

Performing better in the corporate context is all about cost. Corporations want to know how they can do more with fewer people and less money. Performing better in a startup environment is about how the company can be better on all fronts. *How can we have a better customer experience? How do we find the best and most creative people to solve problems? How do we create a better environment for our employees?*

What I've found works in leading startups is to organize

peer groups of skilled individuals to solve problems without a hierarchy. The peer group operates as a team, and everyone brings a different set of skills and expertise to the table. People won't be without their biases or preferences—salespeople will want to sell more, product people will want a better product. However, they'll work to fit their areas of understanding together to figure out how best to solve the problem.

But you can't have a motivated team that trusts you as a boss unless you're a good person. Strong character is essential to effective management. Not only is being horrible to people bad for business, it will eat away at you, destroying your conscience at night. I still think about the time when I was twenty-eight and flew up to New York to find out why sales were flat at a company Cereus had purchased. I met with the vice president of sales, a nice guy in his mid-fifties who had decades of experience. I asked him what was going on with the numbers; he responded by telling me about challenges with the product.

"Do you have a business card on you?" I asked after he had finished talking.

He slid one across the table. It said, "Vice President of Sales." I took out my pen and crossed off the "of Sales" part. I handed it back to him and said, "Clearly, you're just a vice president because you haven't sold anything."

He sat there and looked at me, like *Who the fuck is this guy?* It was a prime example of how *not* to treat people.

By the time I landed back in Atlanta, he had already called Jim Logsdon, the president and COO of Cereus. A veteran leader, Jim was the adult supervision at our company. He's one of the best mentors I've ever had. Jim called me into his office to talk about what he termed my "interesting" meeting up in New York. He gave me a great piece of advice.

"There's evolutionary and revolutionary," Jim said. "When you want to be a revolutionary guy who pushes hard instead of letting things take their time, you have to be careful. Lots of people die in revolutions, and sometimes you get shot by friendly fire." Jim paused. "But in evolution," he said, "nobody dies."

## HOW I LEARNED EMPATHY

I wish I could tell you I learned how to be 100 percent empathetic from that experience, but the truth is it was a process, and 9/11 played a key role. I was originally scheduled to be in New York City on September 13, 2001, to raise a new round of funding, but I decided to stay home. Still, we had numerous people from a new company we had acquired on the ground in New York when the Twin Towers fell. I was in our chairman's office putting fundraising documents together when we turned on CNBC. I thought it was a hoax at first.

My then-wife worked for Delta at the time, and after they sent her home, she called me.

"Don't stop for gas on the drive home under any circumstances," she said.

I was confused about why. Did she have inside information about terrorists coming to Atlanta because of her connection to the airline?

Then I realized I was a brown man in Atlanta. No matter how American I was, it didn't matter.

Before 9/11, I'd always joked that I was a coconut: brown on the outside, white on the inside. I grew up in Stone Mountain, Georgia, an Atlanta suburb with a history as a hotbed for the Ku Klux Klan. As kids, my friends and I would run around the woods and play not only cowboys and Indians, but also Rebels vs. Yankees. I was so assimilated, I would get upset when the kids made me play a Yankee and I didn't get to wave the Confederate flag. I didn't know any better.

After 9/11, I'd get on a plane and the other passengers would look at me funny. I had always grown a beard every winter, but my friends made me stop. I was experiencing racism for probably the first time in my life. Sure, 9/11 affected my business; it accelerated layoffs. But the biggest way it affected me was I learned what it was like to be "the other." That was the real beginning of empathy for me. I eventually developed the ability to treat the people I worked with well. It didn't happen all at once, but over time, and culminating with my pretirement, I learned aggressive stances aren't helpful and fill you with regret.

People often want to know the how-to when it comes to responding with empathy to your employees. I like to say workers should be treated not like your own kids or family members, but like your best friend's kids. There's a different kind of care and responsibility when you're trusted with someone else's children. Even if you love them deeply, there's a level of emotional distance and less of an impulse to be harsh when they misstep. Treating workers like other people's kids will help prevent you from being pissed off at everyone as well as prevent everyone from being pissed off at you.

When you start treating people well, you have to be prepared for mistrust. Nearly everyone is used to mean, narcissistic bosses, so they'll analyze your kindness to find the catch. I once had an employee who was having a rough time both at work and in his personal life. One day, I said to him, "You seem knotted up, and you never find time for yourself. How about you take the afternoon off? Don't go home and get caught up in family life. Go hit a bucket of golf balls. Go watch a movie. Go get a massage. Just go do something."

After I left the room, my assistant told me the guy thought he was in trouble. He was sure I wanted him to clear out so I could box up his stuff before letting him go. I had never treated him poorly, but his response was an indication of how he'd been treated in the past and what he'd come to expect.

## AN ALTERNATIVE TO HR: GETTING TO KNOW PEOPLE

Another way to demonstrate empathy is to ask people questions and listen to the answers. Of course, founders are busy trying to run companies and create shareholder value, but that doesn't mean we can't take time to have authentic interactions with the people making our goals happen. Connecting with them requires us to slow down. I strive to discover what the people who work for me are passionate about, whether it's poetry, knitting, or organic gardening. During job interviews, I ask potential hires what they're passionate about outside of work. Nick, a candidate for a mechanical engineering position, told me in his job interview he was a competitive archer. Most mechanical engineers I've met are interested in sitting permanently behind a desk. The fact Nick had such an interesting pursuit was compelling to me, and I hired him.

Nate was a young guy who worked for me; I ran into him one night at a charity event I attended with my kids—a graffiti event where you paid for a can of paint and made graffiti on the walls and on junk cars. It included fire dancers, music, and a food truck. Nate was volunteering by photographing the event. After chatting, later I learned he spent weekends hacking cars, creating art projects, and building every creative thing he could imagine. He even wore a digital helmet that he called his "TV head." I realized why I had originally hired him: because I knew he was the type of person I wanted to be around. If I could get Nate as passionate about what was important for my company as he was about his side projects, everything would work out.

Meanwhile, it's often difficult to know what's really going on in people's lives in a work environment. Dana Barrett was a buttoned-up Cornell grad who worked for me years ago after Cereus acquired her company. She became a vice president of software development and was in charge of managing a team I had previously hired. Dana came from a suit-and-tie culture; the developers now under her were tattooed and pierced hackers without college degrees. One was even an ex-con.

Dana and I fought every day. She complained the team she was now leading didn't respect her. I responded it was Dana's lack of leadership that was the problem. We ended up hating each other. She eventually left the company, and I don't even remember saying goodbye. Years later during my pretirement, I heard Dana on the radio one day. She now had her own show, focused on technology. We made plans for lunch, and it was amazing how well we clicked. I found out when we worked together, Dana had been a recently divorced single mom with constant stress in her life. As a high-flying guy in my twenties, I had different priorities. Today, we're such close friends we talk nearly every day. If I had known what Dana had been going through, it may have made me a much better boss.

We make all kinds of assumptions about people when we know only a thimbleful of their stories. But if you have connection and caring, you can, often easily, hire the right employees (and manage them well), even if you don't have an HR department. The added benefit is the people working for you know you see them as three-dimensional, instead of as a cog in your machine.

# CHAPTER FIVE

# Leverage Great Relationships

—

After years of being an entrepreneur, I've learned a hard truth: We are not calling the shots. The universe is.

People who become entrepreneurs were often at the mercy of someone else's authority in previous work environments. Once they strike out on their own, there's a tendency to become intoxicated with the newfound freedom and power. They believe executing on a plan—whether it's to hit a milestone or raise your next round—is all it takes to make that plan happen. This sense of control isn't real because there are too many moving parts.

Navigation in the startup world is less about having street-by-street, turn-by-turn directions, and more about having a compass. Roadblocks that are out of your control continually pop up, and sometimes, you hit a dead end. I've found, however, there's always more than one way to get where you're going.

In 1997 at The Reddy Group, the first product my partner and I built focused on engineering and construction management via the web. Engineering and construction were what we knew, and we wanted to create solutions for those industries, which were dysfunctional and difficult to organize. Mistakes are expensive, often brutally so. We invested a huge amount of time and energy in our product, but the world of technology wasn't what it is today. You couldn't whip out your iPhone, take pictures, and send the photos to the cloud.

We knew the industry, we knew what we were doing, we had a plan, but guess what happened when we went to market? Not enough people had computers—some of the companies we approached had one or two computers total. Believe it or not, people still thought the internet was a fad that would come and go, like laser discs. Peyton and I had borrowed against our credit cards to start the company, and we eventually realized we had no idea what we were doing. Fortunately, we were able to pivot. We sold the product to other industries such as telecommunications. But for too long, we were stuck thinking we had it all figured out and were trying to market to the industry we thought we knew.

## THE ANTIDOTE TO EGO: BEGINNER'S MIND

When you believe you are in charge, your ego gets rolling like a snowball down a hill, becoming bigger and bigger. You fall into the trap of thinking everyone around you is stupid. But startups are about experimenting to figure things out. Nothing is known.

Many people come to startups from top companies like McKinsey, the global management and consulting firm; there, they were heavy hitters at sales and driving business. As entrepreneurs, they're shocked when they don't have the same results. At big companies, however, the sales often come to you via phone. In a big corporation, you're running around the decks of a battleship. In a startup, you're in a rowboat. You're beaten by storms and waves, trying to figure out in which direction to go and how to survive.

Brian worked at the accounting and consulting firm Ernst & Young for fifteen years; it was his first job out of college. When he first came to work for me, he did a great deal of predictive modeling, such as building spreadsheets that showed phoning a thousand people about purchasing a product would yield one hundred prospects, and out of that group ten would buy. I pointed out it was all fiction. Brian thought he had driven a large number of sales at E&Y, but he hadn't made a single call himself. His sales all came via referrals from colleagues in his company. He didn't grasp startup life until I laid it out that he was the one who needed to make the one thousand calls.

My advice is if you're founding or going to work at a startup, you should behave like you're straight out of college. Act as if you know nothing. Get comfortable forgetting what you know and starting your career from scratch. In Zen, they call it beginner's mind.

## WHO REALLY HOLDS THE LEVERAGE

If founders aren't in control or in charge, who then has leverage over you? Your investors, partners, employees, and customers.

### INVESTOR LEVERAGE

The holy grail of a startup is getting investor funding, but many people mistake an investor's money for their own. Numerous entrepreneurs don't digest the consequences of taking that money. In the corporate world, the connection between your work and the shareholders' interest is extremely distant. In the startup world, the investor is a constant presence. They typically own more of the company than you do. They're calling; they're engaged; they look at your numbers monthly, if not weekly. They "help" you hire employees, consultants, and law firms. They question your every decision and offer advice and direction. If you don't listen, investors may take your company away from you.

In addition, when the going gets tough, you're often on your own. With RCMS, I had investors who also were in real estate. When the market crashed in 2007 and 2008, they weren't available to help me raise more money; they had their own problems. I was a blip. They told me if I had a problem it was my fault because I should have seen it coming.

Kevin Sandlin is a colleague who worked for a CD-ROM startup back in the day called Adam Software that focused on human anatomy and biology. The company had a thriving culture, and everything was great until they went public. The company missed its numbers the first quarter and everyone was let go, including Kevin. The bottom line is your investors hold the big stick. Because they're your business partners, you must do everything possible not only to be transparent but to work through ups and downs together. Even with doing all that, you still may find yourself out of a job because of factors beyond your control. Every seasoned entrepreneur has a Plan B in his or her pocket.

## PARTNER LEVERAGE

The partner dynamic is one of the most challenging

relationships in entrepreneurism. You make decisions together, and no one's in charge. It's difficult regardless of whether the company is succeeding or not. It's not unlike the Avengers: in the movies, the superheroes are constantly bickering about something.

Partnerships work best when a duo possesses complementary skill sets. One person sells, the other delivers, for example. Peyton, with whom I created my first startup, was probably the best partner I've ever had. We leveraged each other's talents through a competitive, yin-yang relationship. I'd sell the software and internet services; he'd code all night to provide them. I'd tease him about how he wouldn't have anything to do if it weren't for me, and he'd shoot back the same line.

Friction develops in a partnership when the power dynamic shifts. As our company grew, Peyton and I ran into trouble. I became the front man; when we went public, I became CEO with the lucrative salary. Peyton remained the ops guy. The board treated him as an employee, and he left because he was never viewed as a founder and leader.

If one partner believes a win is selling the company for $100 million, but the other would be happy with $5 million, it's a recipe for disaster. In every partnership, it's crucial to have transparent conversations about goals and objectives in advance and whether they line up. If things take a turn for the worse, it can quickly turn into the blame game where partners fight over who made the bigger contribution. Also, be aware each partner's personal dynamics constantly change. When we started working together, Peyton was single, but my then-wife didn't grumble if I worked all night because she had a demanding job as well. When we had our first child, keeping crazy hours became far more difficult. It was one thing for Peyton to work a hundred hours a week, but another for a new dad to do the same.

I advise partners to remember they are joined solely in a business venture alone; they are not partners for life. It's not a marriage. You have to treat each other respectfully, but also have the freedom to explore other projects on your own. If that's not permitted, frustration sets in. Partners are usually the last to recognize their own power struggles. Employees are the first. Disrespect and struggle between partners disheartens employees and makes them concerned about the future, both of which don't make for a fulfilling and productive workplace environment.

## EMPLOYEE LEVERAGE

When hiring as a founder, one of your goals is to take care of people. A higher level of responsibility to your employees exists when you're leading a startup compared to when you're a leader in a big corporation. The last thing any of us wants is to have someone quit his or her job because they can't pay their bills, or to get divorced because a pay cut creates marriage problems. I used to believe other people were hired only to serve me; if they had difficulties with a pay cut, that was their problem. Now, I'm more concerned with ensuring a job is the right fit for everyone involved. In a corporate job, severance packages and job-placement services create a soft landing for an employee if a position doesn't work out. At startups, there's far less security and far more turbulence; sometimes employees flat out don't get paid.

I'm currently advising a startup that wants to recruit an IBM employee with a current salary of $300,000 a year and pay him $150,000 instead. They're hoping to sell the candidate on the excitement of entrepreneurial life. I'm advising them to ask good questions when it comes to how he is going to be able to afford a 50 percent pay cut. Saying yes to the job won't mean he knows exactly what he's getting himself into.

Brent was a vice president at a multibillion-dollar media company. He was a self-proclaimed intrapreneur—an employee at a big firm who believes he or she runs an internal division like a startup, launching different products. Brent was excited about the possibility of working for a real startup, and after making the rounds, received multiple offers. A number offered Brent a CEO title plus equity that would pay off big if the company went public. Brent came to me for advice about which offer he should take. I told him I thought he should go back to his corporate job, or find another one he liked more because he would be risking too much with a startup.

Brent and people like him who come to me for advice are shocked when I advise them to avoid startups; everyone else has been telling them to jump. But when I lay out the financials, they often take my warning to heart. If an executive is making $250,000 a year at his corporate job, he'll probably take a 50 percent pay cut to work at a startup. Startups often promise a big hire that the company will "probably" have an exit in three years. But of course, there are no guarantees. Let's assume the executive jumps and works at the startup for five years, but it fails. That's $625,000 he lost in salary. "Would you invest over a half-million dollars in a high-risk opportunity?" I'll ask. "I'm not telling you what to do. I'm just doing the math for you." I heard Brent eventually landed a great corporate job.

When hiring, startups aren't always honest about the potential risks involved, and it's a boon for founders to lure a top dog away from a big corporation. Such a hire legitimizes the business, investors love it, and the value of the company usually rises after the press release comes out. The company wins whether or not the new hire is successful. If he or she excels, the startup benefits; if they don't, the person is deemed "too corporate," and their failure is attributed to an inability to adapt to startup culture.

As a founder, it's also critical to remember employees are continually trying to adjust to the different stages of a startup. In the beginning, no organizational structure exists. There are usually five to ten people, and consensus rules. Employees tell you what they will and won't do. Since they're with you because they want to be, often making great sacrifices of their time, you're accountable to them. What founders forget is employees expect the company to stay the same way after investors arrive, and that's not feasible.

The next stage involves surfing waves of capital and/or growth, and the waves can get big fast. Employees are either in a position to ride the waves or get pummeled by them. Leaders often forget that as a company evolves, workers become reluctant or even scared to say "no" to any request. That means overwork is a constant. There's a balancing act between obtaining value from employees and pushing so hard they leave. It's important for leaders to check in regularly and find out if employees are happy, because talented people have plenty of other options. One day, they might wake up and decide to leave, and you won't even know why, unless you've been taking stock. Leaders must possess or develop the emotional intelligence to recognize it is difficult for employees to say no in an environment that breeds childlike enthusiasm and rewards go-go-go attitudes.

Leading a startup is tricky because to do so, you must have a personality that inspires people to work for you. You're like Moses telling everyone to follow you across the Red Sea. Yet you also have to be the one looking out for their interests.

## CUSTOMER LEVERAGE

In the early stages of a startup, every customer matters because they are quite literally paying your bills. It's a huge responsibility and a massive source of stress because these customers know you need them. If you have three hundred customers and one leaves, no big deal. If you have three, and one leaves, you may not be able to pay the electric bill.

In addition, early customers yield more clients through referrals, so that increases the pressure to keep them. It always costs more to work with your first customer than what you're making in return, and it takes more time because you don't have processes in place.

The result is, in the beginning, you must be more willing to accommodate special requests and timelines to keep customers. You will likely put in more effort than they're paying you for. For example, Laura is a copywriter who started her own business. She was hired by a firm to write a 250-word blog post for a $500 flat fee. Halfway through the process, the company decided to lengthen the blog post. When Laura complained, the response from the P.R. chief was, "Are you going to nickel and dime me? I thought you were trying to build a relationship with customers." Laura was stuck. She had a car payment coming up. She didn't feel like she could risk losing the five hundred dollars. Her client could just go somewhere else.

In 1997 and 1998, The Reddy Group provided internet access to executive suites (a shared office environment similar to co-working spaces). Because people weren't as internet-savvy as they are now, we would constantly receive tech support calls from landlords whenever a tenant couldn't log on. Often, the solution was as easy as plugging in a cord. But landlords insisted we respond to every tenant request. I was constantly driving a half hour across town to fix a painfully simple problem. It was like being held hostage, but the landlords were our first customers in this arena, so I had to do it.

## WHAT HAPPENS WHEN YOU BURN A BRIDGE?

Striving for startup success, entrepreneurs often find themselves sacrificing relationships along the way. Founders don't start out being unethical, but that's what happens.

They string along vendors or stiff them. They sign on customers but don't deliver. They don't pay their law firms on time. When RCMS fell apart in 2008, I owed millions to people who trusted me.

Rick was one of our clients at RCMS. He was a nice guy in his mid-fifties who had worked at a real estate development company for years. He hired us to build a series of 3-D blueprints from construction drawings. Rick had a deadline, and we told him we'd make it, even though in reality we knew it was unrealistic, given our workload. Deadline arrived. Rick came to our office, reviewed the deliverables, and pointed out the errors in the half-baked job we'd executed. When we told him we'd need two additional weeks, Rick's face crumpled; his stress was evident. He stepped out of the conference room to call his boss. When Rick returned, he was crying. He'd been fired for missing the deadline. It was jarring, and I'll never forget it.

When you burn too many relationship bridges, you end up alone. The flames follow you wherever you go. When you need help, there's no one to call. When RCMS crashed, I avoided everyone, sending their calls to voicemail. I was unable to give up the idea that I'd failed as a superhero. Because I couldn't get real with my investors, employees, and vendors, I went radio silent. When I mentor entrepreneurs today, I remind them it's their responsibility to have the money to pay their bills and to meet deadlines and customer responsibilities. My stomach still hurts when I undergo the professional relationship litmus test: someone like Rick with whom I burned a bridge pops up on LinkedIn as a suggested contact. I've learned, at the end of the day, personal credibility is all I—or any of us—have. It's one of the few things of which we are in charge.

## LONELY AT THE TOP: THE PARADOX

Even when business is going well, startup entrepreneurs nearly always feel alone because everyone constantly turns to you for good news. Investors want to know profits are climbing. Employees want to know their jobs are secure. Customers want to know you can deliver on time. The problem is, for a founder, this creates a plague of fake positivity. During the worst times at RCMS, I always told people the company was doing great. Fake positivity leads to unintended but avoidable consequences, as it did with Rick.

Today, now on the other side, my goal is to leverage great relationships with everyone involved in my startups. I've discovered the following four ways to do that.

* Be truthful.
* Be authentic.
* Keep everyone well informed.
* Tell people where things stand.

I lay out the big picture with customers: whether I can take something on, whether I have enough smart people on board to succeed, and whether it will cost twice as much as they think. During my tenure at the robotics company, Urban Outfitters approached me about making shirts for the firm. I told them we weren't ready to make an entire shirt, but we could do separate parts. I invited top executives to view an example of what we could do and make their own decision. They were impressed with our transparency. After the meeting, they told us they had enough information to consider working with us and would get back in touch. They also said they were interested in a future project where we could share the risk. We considered the meeting a success. We had both demonstrated our expertise and forged a relationship.

Authenticity allows entrepreneurs to share not only the challenges with investors, employers, and customers but the silver linings. Stress levels drop because when you're upfront with people, they treat you the same way.

# CHAPTER SIX

# Meet Every Person Where They Are

A company in Atlanta was celebrating hitting its revenue goals with a startup happy hour. The place was packed, and everyone was drinking hard. I weaved my way through the crowd to the men's room, where I found two guys snorting cocaine on the sink counter. I wondered: Didn't that go out in the 1980s?

At co-working spots and startup incubators across the country today, kegs, Ping-Pong tables, and people zooming around on scooters abound. The freewheeling lifestyle is what draws many people to startups, and since entrepreneurs are often young and carefree, they write off designing culture as something for big corporations. But culture happens everywhere. It's inescapable. If entrepreneurs aren't careful, they may create a bro/

frat-house culture that isn't what they—or those who work for them—want.

Swearing, dressing down, and making degrading generalizations about others result in a subversive vibe that's not unlike when a kid rebels against his parents. (It's one thing for someone to curse, but another to curse at someone else.) At one of my companies, I had a sales guy who came in every Monday morning sharing naked pictures of the women he'd slept with over the weekend. "Dude," I'd tell him, "I don't need to see anything." I was so worried about being the cool boss, I said nothing.

Many of the people I know and love are recovering alcoholics, and it's challenging for them to work for a startup. When they do, colleagues pay lip service to supporting their sobriety while the culture continues to revolve around alcohol. Meanwhile, many workers over thirty or forty who aren't in recovery still don't want to drink themselves into a stupor with twentysomething colleagues. A friend in her forties in this predicament hands the bartender a hundred-dollar bill at the beginning of the night and tells him that no matter what anyone else orders for her, she only wants soda water. Yet she's still hounded by colleagues and deemed a party pooper. Men demand to know if she's not drinking because she's pregnant. That's not OK.

## IS PARTY CULTURE A SYMPTOM OF SOMETHING ELSE?

Drinking isn't evil. But a culture that revolves around drinking, weed, and Ping-Pong isn't a viable, long-term work environment. It's a symptom of a false belief that building a productive culture doesn't require effort or attention. Replicating a frat house isn't hard—especially when the average startup employee is a single guy who lives alone. But that environment creates deep structural problems with running a company. As a founder, if you can't make payroll, but you're gathered around the keg with your staff on a regular basis, there's a problem.

That said, there is a powerful upside to the camaraderie of startup life. In the corporate world, HR policies make it difficult to truly get to know people. An electric fence exists between people's personal and professional lives. Sterile patter is the norm.

"How was your weekend?"

"Crazy with the kids; we had a barbecue. How was yours?"

The beautiful thing about start-up culture is it's rarely superficial. You get to know people well. You often spend more time with them than with your own family. Deep conversations are the norm, as are close relationships. I've made nearly all my close friends through work. When you develop strong connections with people, you're also less likely to judge them. I work with people whose politics are different from mine, but as long as they respect the dignity of others, it's not a problem.

Close connections create a buffer when life gets difficult. Arrol is a former investor who became a close friend and remained so, even after he stole a couple of my employees. When I first told him about my divorce, he immediately insisted we meet for coffee. He counseled me, advising a move to a new neighborhood for a fresh start. He offered to help me hunt for apartments. After I found a place, he stopped by and hung out with my kids, pointing out to them all the benefits of my new apartment complex. If we had met each other in a corporate environment, I doubt he would have felt comfortable offering so much support.

When I look around my office around 5 p.m., I'm struck by the community-family vibe. My kids are often doing their homework; my girlfriend is usually there as well doing her own work and fielding random homework questions. Colleagues are stopping by to say hello and occasionally acting as a Shark Tank panel for my sons' startup ideas. My kids are experiencing what it's like to be part of a caring and learning community, and nothing is more fulfilling to me.

## WHY MILLENNIALS ARE DRAWN TO STARTUP CULTURE

What millennials understand (and what my sons likely do, too, even as teenagers), is life isn't all about work. Punching a clock isn't interesting. Millennials want to bring their authentic selves to work every day, not fake personas. The freedom of startup culture provides more of the authenticity they crave. That's why building a culture that inspires and motivates people, and where they can do good work, is essential.

Designing a culture requires you to be deliberate. My suggestion is to be clear about your core tenets and stick to them daily. For example: A core tenet of treating others the way you want to be treated means you don't yell at people. Ever. As I mentioned in the last chapter, one of our key tenets at The Combine is we are not a teaching organization but a learning one. I'm clear I need people to be engaged and ask questions, but no one has time to teach. Yet everyone has room to fail, and I budget time and money for that.

The benefit of a startup is it is malleable and nimble. You can change a frat-house culture into one of acceptance. It's possible to have a work environment that is both casual and respectful. I try and create that every day. Sometimes, I succeed; other times, I don't. One of my startup employees, Tony, came out to me. He worked up the courage to do so only after he had drunk large amounts of alcohol at one of my annual cookouts for employees. I had thought I'd known Tony well and had been not only a great boss but a good friend. Yet while I had been telling myself we were part of one big family, Tony had been clocking my reactions to missed deadlines or sales targets. As a result, he had been scared to reveal he was gay. When he finally did, he was worried I might fire him (really). Of course I didn't, and of course, I support who he is without question. Tony and I continue to be great friends, and he's come to work with me at subsequent startups. He has been a massive influence on my life.

To be a great leader, you need to explore and challenge your idea of who you are versus the reality. Just because you feel like you're doing all the right things from the playbook of building a healthy culture (like throwing cookouts), it doesn't mean it comes off as consistent or authentic, or that you've truly earned your employees' trust. It's your behavior in the worst of times that demonstrates how people see you.

How do you identify the gap between your impression of yourself versus the reality? It's not easy, and I'm constantly working on it. One way is to ask employees for an honest assessment of their happiness levels at work and not get defensive when you don't like it. Their feedback is more important than their approval. Another is recognizing that approaching a boss with a problem is difficult and stressful on an employee, regardless of the optimism and openness you try to convey. To build a culture of acceptance and respect, you have to focus on figuring out what you can do to help them through an issue. "I can never promise 100 percent happiness," I tell my employees, "but let's shoot for 90 percent. What can I do to contribute?"

As a leader, you must work to find the balance between leading people and making them feel safe enough to trust you to open up. I've learned one key is staying engaged, even when there's no active decision to be made. Engagement builds trust. Another key is to discover what a person's true mission is, and understand that while it may not be yours, the two can overlap. Katie interviewed for a position with my robotics company. I thought she'd be an asset, but she was initially lukewarm about the job. In the course of our discussion, Katie told me her real dream was to be an astronaut. I asked her what experiences she thought she would need to land a position at SpaceX. She said she wanted to expand her abilities to include hands-on engineering experience. Many engineers sit in a cube all day designing things on a computer. Katie, instead, wanted to immerse herself in the technical side of robotics, from building to sautering. After she outlined her desires, I told Katie I'd do everything possible to align the job with her vision. She decided to come on board.

David, a long-term employee of mine, came and told me

he wanted to leave my company. I had no idea why. All he said was one of our portfolio companies had offered him a position, and he was going to take it. I didn't think the move would be good for David and wanted to find out what prompted it. As we talked, I learned he had recently returned from a trip to Europe, and as a result, now had a long-term goal of moving to Barcelona that he thought the new job would help facilitate. Eventually, David decided to work for one of my other startups in the United States, but the job met his desire for change and growth.

## FIVE WAYS TO BUILD A THRIVING CULTURE

Additional ways of building a culture of acceptance and respect include:

* Sharing experiences.
* Doing activities together during personal time.
* Feeling compassion for employees as fellow human beings.
* Overcoming the corporate urge to play games.
* Keeping matters transparent and overcoming the fear that transparency will be used against you. (For example, if you can't make payroll, many employees will hang in there if you simply tell the truth.)
* Building a culture is an art, not a science. Leadership thrives when the people you work with know you support not only their next promotion or job switch,

but what they want out of life and who they want to become.

# CHAPTER SEVEN

# Learn from Your Juniors

———

A colleague recently complained to me about millennials; he's from Generation X like me.

"They want to bring all of their personal life to work with them!" he ragged. "You can't ask, 'How was your weekend?' without hearing about their weekend. It's exhausting!"

For decades, people learned how to conduct mindless small talk in the workplace to avoid having real conversations about their lives. Millennials are breaking the pattern. They talk about who they are and what they're going through. "I didn't get that project done because I was feeling depressed." While millennials do have their problems and weaknesses, such as living vicariously through social media, when it comes to human interaction, they are far more authentic than any other generation.

## PREDICTABLE BIAS

People who work for startups will always possess different backgrounds, histories, cultures, and generations. It's unwise to paint any one group with a broad brush, but I have found distinct differences characterize millennials. For example, they believe you hired an individual, not a position. Is it the worst thing for a person to want to give a piece of themselves to their work? I don't think so.

The big picture is that older generations often resist change because it might affect their way of life. Pre-World War II generations thought baby boomers were selfish and lazy, especially hippies and the "Me" generation. Baby boomers thought Gen Xers were slackers addicted to MTV. Now, boomers and Gen Xers complain about millennials being self-involved.

The battle with millennials, in my opinion, is largely based on jealousy. Millennials create companies, they're well traveled, they're more tech-savvy, and they're guided by an internal compass. Millennials drink craft beer, fly to music festivals around the country, and curate exciting-looking lives online. They're more idealistic. They go for their dreams. They get married and have kids later, giving themselves more time to be happy-go-lucky and work on themselves. They also job-hop as a way of life. I wouldn't say millennials are less materialistic than baby boomers or Gen Xers, but they focus on quality—or at least perceived quality. That can go to extremes. I grew up buying Irish Spring and Dove soap that cost $3 for a five-pack. Today, millennials I know stock up on goat's milk-and-honey artisanal soap at ten bucks a bar. Why? It's simple: they'd rather support a local business at their farmer's market than a big corporation like Unilever or Colgate-Palmolive.

## MILLENNIALS SEIZE THE DAY

Instead of being frustrated by millennials, why don't we learn from them? A fortysomething friend called me the other day for advice on whether she should switch jobs. She was worried how it would look on her resume. Millennials rarely think about such optics. If anything, they believe multiple job changes demonstrate they're aggressively moving forward with their careers and picking up diverse experiences. A Gen Xer with a mortgage, car payments, and kids often becomes bitter toward such a stance—especially if he or she was working nights and weekends paying their dues at the same age.

I was at a dinner recently for a large consulting firm, and the chief culture officer was seated next to me at the table.

During our conversation, the topic of this chapter came up. "Help me to understand," he said. "I have a son-in-law who got a master's in electrical engineering, and then he went to work as an electrical contractor wiring houses. Why?"

I tried to explain millennials aren't defined by degrees. Someone with a fine arts degree might become a software developer. A person with an engineering degree might become a barista. You aren't going to lure the majority of millennials to your company with signing bonuses and a commission structure. You have to provide a context that's meaningful to them. My own pretirement was inspired by this generation. I asked myself, "Why should I wait until I'm eighty to do what I want to do?"

In addition, millennials not only teach people like me to seize the day, they also teach us how to have better relationships. I've found millennials tell it like it is. Deceit, in my experience, is not in their DNA.

## CONNECT AS AN EQUAL

As a leader, how you communicate with millennials is pivotal for building rapport. Even if a significant age difference exists, it's important to remember you're not a parent or a sibling. Your job is to align with them as an equal. As far as hiring, my advice is to take your time. Don't rush to hire too many candidates simultaneously, and don't assume three interviews are enough to know whether a person is the right fit. Also, keep in mind millennials need to participate as part of a team. Individual achievement usually isn't as important as group effort. This is the participation-trophy generation.

The most successful way to hire a millennial, or to inspire them once they're part of your company, is to align with his or her sense of purpose. Tapping into the energy of their passion and directing it toward your mission will bring out the best in a person. The surest way to lose a potential millennial hire is to say, "Put your nose to the grindstone and pay your dues."

Emily was another employee at my robotics company. She was passionate about fashion, young designers, and pop-up events. During our initial job interviews, she struggled with the idea of working in robotics. "It wasn't her thing," she said.

"When it comes to being a young designer," I asked, "what do you think are the biggest challenges?"

"Getting your name out there," Emily immediately replied, "along with getting investors and being able to buy in the right quantities."

"If we can get our robots to work," I said, "and a robot ends up being able to build small batches of product, wouldn't that help a young fashion designer, because she won't have to order in quantities of one million from China?"

Emily's face lit up. She agreed it would. I proposed were she hired, Emily create a community around such a mission. I also told her if extra time became available on nights and weekends, she could bring young designers into the lab to create. Emily became excited about the possibility of robotics empowering up-and-coming designers and growing their businesses in ways that weren't possible before. Suddenly, the company mission was aligned with her personal mission, and she decided to come work for us.

I've found the myth that millennials are lazy ignores what they have to offer. Instead, it's a sign that critics are too attached to their own biases. Millennials are evolving our workplaces to become less hierarchal and impersonal and more human and decentralized. We always have something to learn from someone else, even—and maybe especially—if they're younger than us. By slowing down and checking our emotions, we can avoid the pitfall of thinking we know everything there is to know.

CHAPTER EIGHT

# Build Trust with In-Person Encounters

In the startup world, trust is essential. Because everything moves at warp speed, decisions must be made with incomplete information. Big risks are taken daily. Without trust, nothing would ever happen in a startup.

I believe trust has two parts: emotional and intellectual. Emotional trust is about integrity and putting your faith in others; intellectual trust is about logic. As leaders, emotional trust occurs when people are open or confide in us; it should never be taken for granted. When emotional trust is violated—such as using personal information for leverage in a Machiavellian way—the results are devastating. Emotional trust is built over time and multiple interactions; it's just not going to happen easily over texting or Slack.

In a startup, leaders need to take promises at face value; that's where intellectual trust comes in. If your software developer tells you on Friday he'll have a piece of code for you by Tuesday and doesn't, he wasn't lying. It wasn't a violation of emotional trust. Developers almost always make such promises with earnest intentions; when they don't come through, it's usually due to being inexperienced or overly optimistic. You won't lead effectively if you hold failure over their heads.

Instead, you have to know better and use logic. When an unrealistic promise is made, it's best to leave wiggle room. Build a buffer to let people fail and learn on their own without it negatively impacting your objectives. Sometimes, intellectual trust is about possessing the emotional intelligence to know when to say, "Hey, how can I help you?"

Trust is the first step to being able to take risks as a team. At RCMS, Chris, one of our developers, was writing the code for a piece of analytics software. He was swamped but assured me and our team he had the job handled. We eventually discovered that nearly everything he had done was wrong. Instead of playing the blame game, the team and I banded together and recognized we had put Chris in a position where he was in over his head. We took accountability that we hadn't created an environment where he felt he could ask for help. We had unknowingly set him up for failure. Together, everyone worked nights and weekends to get the project done. That experience caused me to define teamwork in a new way. I'd like people to see teamwork as rallying behind someone not only when things are going great, but when he or she drops the ball. It's about helping people when we lose—not just when we win.

## WHY TECHNOLOGY CAN'T REPLACE IN-PERSON CONNECTIONS

I generally travel about a hundred days a year. It seems absurd in this day and age. But trust is built through in-person encounters. One of my competitive edges is I'm constantly getting on a plane to meet people and maintain personal relationships. Books abound on how to build the right culture in a company, but even with great effort to do so, it's wishful thinking to believe a text or an email is always initially viewed in the most positive light. Human nature doesn't work that way. Plus, many of us struggle to read and absorb emails longer than a paragraph.

Nor does written communication convey the humor, sarcasm, and deeper intentions that face-to-face encounters do. A remark that comes across funny in person can make you look like an asshole in writing. Plus, texts and emails are superb at creating mistrust through misinterpretation. Delays in communication can have someone falsely conclude you're wavering on a decision, ignoring them on purpose, or even hiding something.

Ray is an entrepreneur I've befriended who crashed and burned a few years ago with his company. Relationships with his former colleagues are nearly nonexistent. Ray recently launched a new apparel company and will only communicate with everyone involved via FaceTime. Part of that is his need to be emotionally connected to people, but another is he knows the dangers of emailing and texting. Startups are about people. The opportunity to misunderstand a text/Slack/WhatsApp message due to lack of context is massive and commonplace.

## PRESENCE FOSTERS TRUST

Today, everyone is in a constant hurry to get to the next thing, sacrificing connection for productivity. I learned about slowing down in part from ARC, the company that bought RCMS. The executives and founders treated me like an individual, not someone whose sole worth was based on net value or productivity.

Their philosophy about work was:

* Things take time.
* Don't be in a hurry or move too fast.
* A deliberate pace is best.

As one of my first projects, executives asked me to train approximately four hundred of their salespeople in sixty cities to sell our building information modeling (BIM) software. To do so, I created weekly instructional webinars and held teleconferences. One month later, reports from the satellite divisions showed nearly nonexistent sales. After analyzing the situation, I realized up until now, the salespeople had been marketing printing services—selling banners, blueprints, and the like—to local markets. Their days were filled with on-site visits to hometown clients, where they met staff and schmoozed over the donuts they had brought. The salespeople weren't responding to webinars and teleconferences because they weren't their mode of operation. We needed a different tack.

With my boss's blessing, I hit the road. In the first six months, I traveled to thirty cities, meeting staff face-to-face and training them. I learned once you get to know people, they'll go out of their way to help you. Word began to spread in our offices across the country I wanted them to succeed and would do everything in my power to make it happen. Invites from regional vice presidents poured in. When the six months was over, our sales had quadrupled. Webinars couldn't bring that result. Technology can't create context, which is often what people need in order to make key decisions. In-person encounters allow people to learn the depth of your experience, as well as your background. They provide both facts and personal support.

## BEING AROUND WHEN LIFE HAPPENS

Today, social media tricks us into thinking we're closer to people than we actually are. How many of those friends on Facebook are your real friends? I was in the airport the other day scrolling through posts, and someone from elementary school messaged me, asking how life was going. "Great," I replied.

But we weren't close in second grade, hadn't talked in over thirty years, and probably won't forge a close relationship. We've all had weird Facebook experiences like that, right? Social media also exaggerates how well our lives are going. We're posting pictures of our dinners, vacations, birthdays, and hikes without people knowing who we really are and what's truly going on in our lives underneath the surface.

With personalized interactions, however, you're around when life happens for people. You lend an ear when a colleague's kid doesn't make the soccer team or get into college. You offer counsel and advice when someone's going through a breakup. Being present creates trust. When my girlfriend, my boys, and I eat dinner together, our phones go into a pile until we're done eating. With work or our personal lives, it's not the quantity of time that matters in building relationships, but the quality. Putting the phone away helps me understand what makes people tick and vice versa. The distractions are gone, as is the need for masks.

## TEAM BUILDING

Meanwhile, when teams are geographically close to each other, a teaching and learning dynamic occurs. At RCMS, a silo mentality dominated. We had endless cubicles and offices; all the salespeople were in one area, the developers in another. The environment didn't help the company grow and thrive at the highest levels. It's a different story in an office with an open floor plan and everyone mixed in together. If you're in accounting, and you hear a salesperson at the next desk getting yelled at by a customer over an accounting error, a different dynamic occurs. You're automatically experiencing customer behavior and your own impact, both on the client and your colleague. In addition, when startup leaders are on-site and in the thick of things every day, they learn more about their company and its employees and how to improve both.

Countless startups try to solidify their teams with group activities like golf or tennis tournaments. The problem is someone is always great at those sports, and everyone else is tagging along. Such activities often don't encourage authenticity as much as they do bravado. Many companies default to happy hour for bonding, but as discussed, that creates a drinking culture where not everyone feels comfortable.

Informal, in-person activities *are* important to teams. What's best, however, is to create a level playing field. I gravitate toward pursuits that are on par with elementary school games. With one of my companies, we held an annual field day with three-legged races. At another, we held a hack-o-lantern competition around Halloween; teams made up of engineers, accountants, and HR people created 3-D printed jack-o-lanterns. People come in all shapes and sizes, possessing many different experiences, and such activities allow them to show their strengths and weaknesses in ways they can't in formal business settings. They ultimately help strip away barriers. They allow people to value skills that others bring to the table and to subsequently feel comfortable later asking for help with work-related challenges. It's difficult to reach out to people with whom you have only a work relationship.

A couple years ago, I decided to give my son a skateboard for Christmas, but I didn't want to buy one retail. I approached Nate Damen, one of my employees, and asked him if he'd help me make one. We bought a plate of aluminum and built one together. While Nate did most of the work, it was a great experience that brought us closer as human beings.

## WHAT HAPPENS WHEN YOU'RE NOT IN A ROOM

Decision makers, like investors and customers, also thrive in an atmosphere of trust, and staying geographically close to them facilitates it. When RCMS was bought by

ARC, I commuted from my home in Atlanta to their California office regularly. My new board and chairman were thrilled with the acquisition, and our working relationship flourished.

When I hit the road training salespeople around the country, however, our relationship grew distant and eventually strained. It became easy for leaders to rethink my vision and change previously discussed plans, often without consulting me. Relationships are not one and done; they need to be tended, nurtured, and maintained. If you're not in the room, not at lunches, and not looking people in the eye, eventually a bond frays...and breaks. Unfortunately, when times get tough, it's easy for people to forget your value. In my case, my decision makers lost confidence in my vision and began to cut back on their investment in me. When I received an offer from Gehry Technologies (architect Frank Gehry's technology company), they agreed to release me from my contract early.

When it comes to your own presence as a startup leader and change maker, I've found it's easy for entrepreneurs to forget about the importance of their emotional and physical presence to those who work for them. Staying connected to your employees often takes huge amounts of time and energy, far more than you may feel you have to give. But it's critical. You've got to be there.

People are naturally resistant to change, and doubt grows among staff when you're far away. Relationships can't be fostered and nourished if you're a moving target. It's not unlike romantic relationships.

As everyone knows, startups are volatile, and when it's not going well, people begin fighting over resources. Whether you're a founder or a top player, there's always a finite pile of money, and if you're not in the room to fight your fight, you won't be at the table. FaceTime or Skype won't cut it, and you can't send a hologram in your place.

## RELATIONSHIPS ARE THE END GAME

Over the years, I've developed multiple ways to foster in-person time with my employees and colleagues. For starters, as a leader, it's not difficult to sense when people are unhappy or lost. I've learned you've got to choose to pull your head out of the sand (or not stick it there in the first place). When I sense disharmony in someone with whom I'm working, I invite them for a walk or coffee. It's amazing what a twenty-minute break does for relationship building.

I also include people in meetings they might not normally attend, ones even outside their weight class. I might take an engineer with me to a meeting with an investor, for example. Meetings like that create excitement about the company, as well as a sense of belonging. They promote trust and provide a glimpse into my reality. In many start-ups, no one knows what the CEO does. From the outside looking in, everyone I work with might think I spend my time lighting cigars with hundred-dollar bills at wine bars. Bringing a staff member into a meeting helps them understand the level of stress involved with being a leader.

Too many startup founders fail to realize building relationships is just as important as budgets and hiring. Connection is also forged through authenticity. In the corporate world, many leaders paste on a false demeanor that everything is always going great. If I'm having a bad day, I let my team know, so no one thinks my grumpiness is because of them. It's easy to forget, as a leader, people are scared of you. But if we're mutually engaged, fear dissipates. Such a bond becomes essential when your staff undergoes a serious event, such as a breakup or a death in their family. If you haven't formed a solid relationship, you'll be ill-equipped to offer support—and for it to be perceived as authentic.

Support goes both ways. Recently, I was tapped out of ideas for solving a dilemma with one of my companies. Maybe it's because I watched so much *MacGyver* and *The A-Team* as a child of the 80s, but normally, I always have a sense for how to get out of a mess. I confided in a team member, and he pointed out my travel schedule was crazy. He suggested I was spreading myself too thin. He was right. Because we had a pre-existing relationship, he knew intuitively my struggle was about more than needing a good night's sleep. And because of our long-term relationship, I was able to weigh what he said. I cancelled the rest of my work trips for the last few weeks of summer and hung out with my kids before school started.

Because of the opportunity to forge meaningful relationships through working at startups, those relationships shouldn't be tied to the rise or fall of any one venture. I like to look at a company as one game in an entire season. You might lose (if the company fails), but you still have other games to play. If you desire, you and your teammates can go on and work together at other companies in the same way actors in one movie go on to work with each other in another. Or, you can part ways with no acrimony.

A consultant I currently work with was employee No. 3 at my first startup. Back then, we had spectacular fights and went through numerous ups and downs. I had times when I couldn't pay him and one where I was forced to let him go. Our relationship survived because along the way, we forged an authentic connection and learned a great deal from each other. Because of shared trust, our relationship isn't dependent on any one venture's success or failure.

In the end, life is less about the work and more about the

relationships you have. One of the biggest benefits to building trusting relationships is how happy it makes your work environment. Work has been highly demonized for most of us. We grow up thinking it's soulless and boring, and it doesn't help when you dislike your co-workers and dread seeing them every day. When we work with great people, they become family. Trust helps us understand what we're getting into and how to scale the challenges together. I realize when you picked up this book, you may have had a different definition of what it meant to be an entrepreneur. My hope is I've been able to provide a new paradigm, one where being an entrepreneur is less about the company than about how you are going to evolve and grow, and how you help everyone around you to do the same.

# PART THREE

# *Business Practices That Bring Sanity*

# CHAPTER NINE

# Keep Perspective When You're Running Lean

In my early startups, I used to believe I needed to hold up the universe, and everything was about *me*. If people quit, it was about me. They didn't like me, so they were morons. If the company didn't do well, it was my fault, and I blamed myself incessantly for failing to see the hazards or roadblocks. At a certain point, however, I realized when my efforts succeeded, it wasn't the result of my work alone. That meant when things failed, it wasn't 100 percent my fault either. Sometimes, shit happens. I didn't cause the economy to crash in 2008. I didn't work at Goldman Sachs or approve subprime mortgage loans.

As entrepreneurs, we often tie our egos to our companies,

especially if the companies are formed from our own ideas and concepts. It's a heavy burden when we're too attached to successful outcomes, particularly if it's an entrepreneur's first time as a CEO. When a big corporation misses its numbers, the CEO rarely personalizes the poor outcome. He points to all the external factors that affected the business such as rising interest rates. He usually doesn't discuss his role or responsibility in the situation. He's been coached to know and demonstrate that he's doing the best he can with the resources he has. But startup CEOs who are making much less money and possess far fewer resources take *all* the responsibility for a bad outcome.

Instead, startup CEOs need to give themselves a break because they're nearly always operating with limited information. My advice is to stop blaming yourself and look for what you can learn from challenges and failures.

Aumri was an intern who was about to be hired on to my company full time. We gave him a project: email every prospect who had signed up for a new system and request a fifteen-minute meeting to discuss customer satisfaction. However, Aumri didn't receive specific directions from our team, and with the best of intentions, he went rogue.

I was in Chicago at a conference when the shit hit the fan. After finishing a speech, I looked down at my phone and saw seven missed calls from Aumri. Working from home without our knowledge, Aumri had logged onto our system, downloaded all our prospects' personal information, and sent out hundreds of emails without using a blind cc. Every prospect's email was visible to the group. Many were furious. As a result, we were at risk for being sued for violating privacy.

Instead of blaming and firing Aumri, I looked for the learning opportunity. We educated Aumri on the dangers of working on his own without our knowledge and sending communications containing sensitive information without a second set of eyes reviewing it. As leaders, we looked at how our own instructions were incomplete and how that led to the result. We committed to it never happening again and decided to personally call everyone on the list and apologize. The vice president of marketing sent out an official apology email himself, and to level the playing field with our prospects, he included his personal cell number and email address.

I was frank with my board about what had happened. I described running a startup as akin to running with scissors. Sometimes, we nick ourselves, but sometimes, we fall right on the blade. It's the risk that comes with the territory, and the best we can do is make sure when we fall, we don't hit a major artery. Startups are always under-resourced and running lean. As a result, balls get dropped.

Things fall through the cracks. You can't be shocked if something breaks.

In a corporate setting, I never would have been able to talk to my board that way. A corporate mentality says:

1. Cover your ass.
2. Shit rolls downhill.
3. Blame the decision maker.

No benefit would have come from yelling at Aumri. Even though he screwed up, Aumri was still a brilliant guy and a great hire. If you fired a quarterback for every bad pass, you'd never have a team. All I can do as a leader is learn from failure the way airlines do from the black box after a crash. If I've hired the best employees and the right people are on my board, I can focus on solving the next problem.

## WHAT WORKS? A HUDDLE

One evening, I was judging a high school pitch competition as part of my work as chairman of TiE, a global nonprofit focused on entrepreneurship. The event was similar to Shark Tank; kids would come on stage and introduce themselves to a panel before pitching a fictional startup. Nearly every kid proclaimed he or she was the CEO or CFO. I don't want to sound patronizing, but I don't think that's how startups should work. I never had a title at my first startup. I didn't think I'd earned one. Titles are, for the most part, irrelevant. Of course, you can make it clear if you're a founder, but you have to earn a CEO title. That doesn't happen for a while. Work tends to go badly in startups if people believe their title dictates what they do and nothing more.

The corporate world is comprised of silos: one person works in operations, another in finance, and so on. You do this, I do that. In a startup, everyone is doing *everything*. Startups excel when everyone views himself or herself as part of a team focused on solving problems. A silo mentality has to go out the window; you can't see yourself as solely in sales or solely a developer. What works instead is a classic football huddle where everyone checks their egos to focus on winning the game. I always tell founders they are quarterbacks, not team owners or head coaches. A quarterback may lead, but he still needs to earn everyone's respect and value their knowledge. If the wide receiver knows another play would work better, he should listen. Classic football movies show what happens when a quarterback acts like a prima donna: blockers step out of the way and let him get pounded. It's not that different in the startup world. Quarterbacks and founders need to play team ball, or they're toast.

## ATTITUDE AND APTITUDE

When smart, highly motivated people of different backgrounds and disciplines operate as a unit, magic happens. There's no need or room for a blame game. My experience is startups succeed when the people who work for them possess two qualities: attitude and aptitude.

With attitude, a person says, "I'll do whatever it takes. Just tell me what needs to happen."

With aptitude, it's, "I'll do whatever is required, but I've never done that before. Will you show me how?"

One of my first hires at RCMS was John Catalano. John was a computer-aided design technician for an RCMS client. He was a motorcycle-driving New Yorker living in the South, a former sound engineer for '80s rock bands like Twisted Sister. John had never written code. The most he'd done with the internet was set up his company's router. But he was passionate about what we were doing. He wanted to be a part of RCMS, so we hired him. He taught himself to write code. He learned to sell. He was always learning something new, and no matter what you asked him to do, the answer was, "Yeah, man. No problem." That's an example of stellar attitude and aptitude. (John still works with me today, and I'm lucky he does.)

A CEO needs to constantly assess everyone on his or her

team for attitude and aptitude levels. It's a balancing act: Someone with a bad attitude but amazing aptitude is awful to work around. Someone with great attitude but no aptitude is counter-productive. It's tricky because when it comes to hiring in a startup, you generally can't afford people with the best attitude *and* the highest aptitude. The answer is to try and hire those who can grow and stretch into new roles. Bring in hires who are coachable and willing to learn—millennials are brilliant at upping their aptitude through YouTube videos and Quora. Also, I've learned as a leader that it's easier to torpedo someone's attitude than to bring it up, so take care to treat people well.

Improving aptitude is tied to creating a culture of honesty. In a startup, there's rarely time to send someone to a class to get up to speed. The result is not everyone's going to have the answers all the time. If employees feel free to tell you when they're stuck, and they'll try and solve a problem anyway, then you have the opportunity for both a solution and for people to increase their aptitude. A culture of honesty is critical for entrepreneurial survival. In a startup, every hour counts and resources must be prioritized. If an employee makes a promise to deliver and can't—either because they were scared to tell you the truth or lacked the aptitude—trouble follows.

Instead of blaming others when things go wrong, I've found the following route more effective:

* Analyze why things didn't work out.
* Do something different in order to move forward.
* Move forward as a team.
* Recognize you succeed or fail together.

## STARTUP CEOS MUST TAKE RISKS

In the corporate world, CEOs are rarely allowed to make decisions. Instead, they must seek buy-in for a decision the company has usually already made. CEOs lay out the choices and guide colleagues and staffers toward the one most favorable to the company's goals. In doing so, they attempt to get people engaged and excited about a matter in which they have no say and often know it. If the initiative falls apart, no one gets fired because everyone agreed on it. But often because such decisions lack risk, the company can't evolve or grow to its highest potential.

For example, a global soft drink giant hired me to judge one of their internal hackathons. (The company is based in Atlanta where I live; you can probably put two and two together as to which firm it is.) Sales were declining with the flagship diet soda because people today want more chemical-free drinks. The hackathon's purpose was to figure out how to revitalize the product. Most of the ideas focused on marketing or packaging. One idea proposed adding rainbows to the cans during LGBT Pride Month since research showed gay men loved the product. Another was reducing the six-pack to a four-pack to make it more convenient for dinner.

"What do you think?" the executives asked me of the proposals.

"You're not doing anything," I replied. "You're just going through a process. My advice is to *embrace* the chemicals like Red Bull and Monster are doing. Market the fact that the drink's *not* natural."

My feedback didn't gain any traction because in the end, the hackathon was a show. The company curated it with the startup community; they got people excited about new ideas. Yet the goal was never to introduce something groundbreaking. The hackathon wasn't about ideas or results; it was about creating a spectacle.

If a soft drink startup was losing market share with a diet product, the product would most likely be killed. Something better would be built to replace it. But if the founder came from a corporate environment, the soda could stay, languish, and end up costing the startup valuable time, money, and resources. Why? Because the founder brought a buy-in mentality with them from their former company.

In tandem, since they also believe the buck stops with them, they take too much responsibility for failure or the potential of it. As a result, they limit their risks and often end up feeling stuck and trapped in their leadership role. It's a mindset for misery.

One afternoon in the early days of my robotics company, I told my team, "We're doing something that's never been done before. I think we're well-equipped to do it, but failure is a high probability. We just need to be aware of that."

"What if we do fail?" my CTO asked worriedly.

"We'll just find some other shit to do," I replied. "It won't mean that we're bad at our jobs. It won't mean that we didn't know what we were doing. We'll just move on to the next thing as a team."

My advice for startup CEOs is to release themselves from a mentality that they must stay the course, no matter what. Let go of the archetype of the fearless leader. Instead, listen to ideas and opinions from your team about where to go and how to get there. In a startup, it's always about moving forward—together.

# CHAPTER TEN

# Straighten Out Your Priorities

———

My dad was born in India, in a village where the infant mortality rate was extremely high. He was named Pulla, which translates directly to *sour*. By the time he was born, his mother (my grandmother) had lost a number of children at birth or shortly afterward. Grief and worry were ever-present about losing more. It was common for people then to say, "If you want your babies to live, don't give them good names." One theory was the gods wouldn't want to take away a baby with a bad name. Another was a bad name allowed the mother to stay more psychologically detached.

The latter school of thought resonates with me when I think about how people name their startups. A founder might spend weeks coming up with a name for his or her company. When they finally do, they run straight to 99designs and spend even more time designing a logo. They might not even have a business model, but they already have a psychological attachment to the company. I believe that's the wrong route. I don't want to sound morbid, but like my father's village, the mortality rate in the startup community is extremely high. You're in for a rough time if you become too attached to your company, especially from the get-go. A founder will often say his business is his baby. But that perspective makes it all about you. Your business isn't your baby. It's a name, a tax ID, and a bank account. It's not a human being.

My observation is the more people merge their egos and personalities with their companies, the greater the chance of failure. In addition, companies named too soon often can't pivot with the market: founders fear the name would need to go, or wouldn't translate to customers with the new direction. Instead of viewing your business as your baby, it's better to view your business as a *project*. With a baby, if it's not going well, you can't sell it or give it away. With a project, you can change the idea or the path to success; you can leave it, sell it, or tweak it. With a project, you can even give it up completely, and it's no big deal.

## THE DANGERS OF OVER-ATTACHMENT

RCMS, the name of one of my former companies, stood

for Reddy Computer Marketing Services. I learned the hard way that putting my own name on it was a mistake. As a result, I became too attached to making it a success. I kept trying to save it when the best thing I could have done for myself and everyone else was let it sink. My extreme personal attachment to RCMS was why my health deteriorated to the point where I nearly died.

This kind of attachment blinds startup founders to reality. I remember when the veil was torn off for me at RCMS. I was sitting at my desk around 5 p.m. My office had a great view of Atlanta, and the sun was going down over the city. My phone rang. It was our credit card company. RCMS had a line of credit I'd personally guaranteed, and it was being called in. I had thirty days to pay back a quarter of a million dollars. If I didn't, the credit card company was going to sue me. Not my company, me.

After I hung up, I looked at the company's numbers. They told me what I already knew: even if all our customers paid up immediately, it wasn't enough to pay back the line of credit. The country was in the middle of the economic crisis of 2008, and I had run out of options when it came to finding a lender. I sat at my desk watching employees outside my office heading home. Some popped in to say good-bye. It was awful knowing payroll was coming up, and I didn't have the money to cut their checks. I kept visualizing a process server with court papers ringing the doorbell of my house, and my wife answering it. After everyone left, I eventually broke out a bottle of twenty-year-old Scotch in my desk drawer and got drunk. For a few hours, the panic subsided. Then, another panic surfaced: that of my wife's reaction to me coming home drunk that night.

## OBSESSION

When founders become over-attached to their companies, obsession sets in. Another reason I couldn't let go of RCMS was I was obsessed with proving the doubters wrong. Obsession swallows up any remnant of normal life. You don't exercise or eat right; you boast about living off Soylent like that's a good thing. Personal finances go out the window, as do meaningful relationships. Some of us even lose our hair. All that matters is snagging the next customer, the next investor, the next superstar employee.

Obsession also blinds us to other opportunities. When I was Chief Information Officer at the telecom company Verso, Intel approached me about being on their technology advisory board. Receiving the invitation was a huge honor and a path to helping shape the industry through collaboration with big players. I accepted, and Intel outlined the responsibilities, which included flying out to their headquarters for quarterly meetings. I ended up attending zero meetings. Being on Intel's board would have created countless personal opportunities and provided exposure to key executives. But I couldn't see that because I was too focused on proving myself after Verso went public. I didn't think about the stratospheric professional development working with Intel would have provided. I wish I had.

## THE POWER OF BALANCE

If you had a friend who told you she had a high-stress job harming her health, hurting her finances, and damaging her personal relationships, including her marriage, what would you say if she asked you for advice? You'd probably tell her it was time to leave. But when start-ups put those important parts of our lives in peril, we can't see what we need to do. We don't realize life will not magically get better until we, alone, change our situation. We're addicted to the fantasy, again, that we're in control. But (again), there's no such thing as control. Real success and fulfillment come from playing a long game, where your goal is to continually develop as an individual.

One way to do that is to simply relax and, again, treat your business like one part of your life, not the whole deal. Charlie Paparelli is an angel investor and a good friend in Atlanta. He's always introducing me to people as the most laid-back guy he's ever met. Then he'll add, "I don't even know how K.P. makes money; he's always hanging out without a care in the world." One day, Charlie asked me point-blank how I remain so consistently calm.

I knew Charlie was a Christian, and his faith was extremely important to him. "You of all people should understand," I replied.

"What do you mean?" Charlie said.

"We like to think everything's in our hands, but even if we make all the right moves and do all the right things, dynamics remain out of our control. I only focus on what I can do and let go of the rest."

When I'm relaxed, I stay calm. When I stay calm, a sense of optimism follows. Customers and investors tend to be drawn to optimism, and because of it, they bring me more business. No one wants to be around someone who reeks of desperation. It's like dating: you're always more successful at finding the right person if you're confident, cool, and calm. It's no different with startup life. Finding your center is the starting point in creating a positive cycle.

What many entrepreneurs do instead is don a mask of false optimism in service to pleasing investors and customers. If the business ends up flailing, false truths and embellishments follow to keep up the front. Stress subsequently increases on founders as they struggle to hide the gap between how they're portraying the state of the business and reality. I've found there's no greater stress than trying to keep a lie under wraps. Doing so creates a vibe of desperation, and that can start to repel customers and investors, causing a downward cycle.

Startups possess countless unknown variables, and unfortunately, lying can become a way of life for entrepreneurs. When I ask entrepreneurs how their sales pipeline looks, I often hear a number like $10 million in business is expected within the next year or so. But when I ask what portion is due to sales with real contracts, the answer is usually zero. No one wants to admit they have zero sales.

When you're in a relaxed mode, however, you don't need false optimism and you don't need to lie. When obstacles and challenges surface, you lay out the facts, but people don't tend to freak out because of your manner. Being authentic creates the opportunity to brainstorm together for solutions. An investor might have that missing piece of information you need to jumpstart sales, or he or she might know the right person to introduce you to in order to take the company to the next level.

Being honest and authentic is far easier when you're not overly attached to your company, when you remember it's not who you are, but a project you're working on for the time being. When you hit rough waters as an entrepreneur, try asking yourself, "Do I care more about what happens to my company, or about what happens to my life?"

# CHAPTER ELEVEN

# Have the Courage to Choose Your Personal Life over Business

———

Maybe you, like me, have friends addicted to extreme sports challenges and workouts—twelve-mile Tough Mudder obstacle courses where participants dodge hanging electrical wires; Antarctic Ice Marathons; brutal CrossFit regimes. My friends in their forties and fifties who do this stuff are shocked when they get hurt in the process. I'm not. I want to say, "You're fifty-five years old. Should you really be biking a hundred miles in a day? What's wrong with public transportation?"

Even after one of my friends gets hurt, he rarely slows down. "I'm going to work through my injury," he'll tell me.

"Don't do that," I'll respond. "You need to rest. Let your body heal at its own pace. How about just 'being' for a while?"

He'll look at me like I'm a weirdo. His mentality is he's got to keep pushing. He's got to keep going. It's the same mentality among startups. We've decided collectively as a culture that startups equal pain. If we're not suffering, we must not be doing it right. In order to be a successful entrepreneur, you need to know when to stop. In my companies, if something's extremely difficult or not working, I take it as a sign I need to look for a different, easier way. It's not inaccurate that launching and running startups is hard, but it's wrong to assume that's the way it has to be. Why shouldn't we look for ways to make it easier?

Let's return to the sports analogy. Instead of working through an injury, what if you took three weeks off? Instead of waking up at 6 a.m. every morning and running to the gym, you have breakfast with your kids and take them to school. Your arm heals beautifully and your relationship with your family strengthens. Similarly, consider a couple who are trying to get pregnant but are unsuccessful. Finally, they throw up their arms and say, "Forget it." A month later, the wife is pregnant. There's something mysterious about stopping and pausing and giving yourself a break that creates a positive outcome. Persevering no matter what isn't the optimal path to success.

During my pretirement, I learned a new term: self-care. Before then, my life had solely been about my investors and employees, my significant other, and my kids. I'd get a massage now and then, but I didn't understand the concept of taking care of myself. In pretirement, I started taking baths. You read that right: baths. Before, my attitude was: "Who the hell has time for a bath? They're so inefficient!" But that's exactly why I needed them. While I had always understood the importance of spending quality time with the people who matter to me, in pretirement, I came to realize I was one of those people too. (P.S.: Call me if you want to talk about the best bath bombs.)

Startup culture doesn't talk about self-care. Startup culture glorifies struggle and tenacity. Conversations about perseverance are as ubiquitous as Ping-Pong tables in co-working spaces. Monday Motivational memes at startups are often the exact same ones posted by CrossFit addicts. You'll never learn about entrepreneurial motivation and inspiration from the Twitter feed of someone who has never been in the trenches, no matter how many followers he has. You'll only find it by spending face-to-face time with the real deal.

## CHANGING OUR INNER DIALOGUE

One reason an entrepreneur refuses to quit or step back from startup life is he or she fears being labeled a failure. Most of the time, though, other people don't label us failures; we do that to ourselves. We all have an inner critic who beats us up on a regular basis. Entrepreneurs, especially, are pros at punishing themselves. There's nothing an unhappy board can say to an entrepreneur about a poor performance he or she hasn't already said to themselves in stereo for weeks prior to the board meeting.

I learned how to talk to myself differently after I got divorced. It started when I made a friend on the plane while commuting to California one day. Like me, Casey was in the tech industry, but unlike me, she was grounded in practices to balance the mind, body, and spirit. She introduced me to breathwork, an umbrella term for breathing exercises that help you achieve a deep level of internal balance and healing. Casey also motivated me to change my yoga practice, focusing less on making it a workout and more on finding equanimity in the flow. Over time and especially during pretirement, these two practices—breathwork and holistic yoga—helped me slow down, observe my internal dialogue, and change it when it was harmful and untrue. I learned how to reframe situations. As hard-driving entrepreneurs, we beat ourselves up all the time, personalizing mistakes and punishing ourselves. When a product fails or when a key person quits, we suffer emotional blows because we've made it all about us.

One way to bypass your inner critic is to see yourself through the eyes of a six-year-old. Try imagining how your kids, or those you know if you don't have any, run to greet you when you get home. Those kids don't think you're a failure. They think you're awesome. That's how we need to see ourselves.

Yoga and breathwork might not speak to you. Meditation may cause you to fall asleep. That's OK. We all simply need to discover what works for us to help quiet the mind and view ourselves and our lives differently. Doing so helps us evaluate where we're investing our time and energy on an ongoing basis. Maybe it's hiking, swimming, running, or listening to music for you. One day during pretirement, I decided to get up at dawn, eat breakfast, and sit on my sofa the entire day. My goal was to watch the sun come up and go down from one spot.

"Why would you do that?" my friends asked. "That's insane!"

But it wasn't. It was part of a series of experiments I was running on my mind and body to help me know myself better. I knew I'd be returning to work after a year, and I didn't want to respond to stress or change in the ways I'd done before. I needed to find out how to bring the calm and peace I was experiencing in pretirement back into work. In business, we run experiments all the time to see what does or doesn't work with a product or a process. Why don't we do that more with our own lives?

## STAYING IN THE RIGHT LANE

When we get too enmeshed in startup life, our personal and professional lives often go off the rails because we lose perspective. Based on my own experience, there are questions to ask yourself in service to regaining it.

When it comes to your personal life, try asking yourself if the current state of your relationships is the same as it was before you dived into being an entrepreneur. Am I still spending time with the people I love? Have bonds become more troubled and tense? Is my relationship with my family different than it was before? Am I there for them when they need me? Have I been putting them last? Then, ask yourself about your own inner state. Am I more stressed/angry/sad/depressed? Am I still doing the things for myself that I used to enjoy (golf, hiking, traveling, being with friends)? What have I given up? On an emotional level, do I feel differently about life now than I did before launching my startup?

When it comes to your business, it's essential to look at the trends and indicators in your sector and see if you're on track. How long have I been at this? How far do I have to go? How much more time will it take to get there? Maybe you've pivoted to meet market needs. Have we lined up successfully with the changed vision? Is there anything remaining from what inspired my initial passion? Look at where the business is today. Is this where I'd planned on being? If not, how is it different? Finally, look at the "magic number" that names the price you'd accept to exit. What would I do if I sold the company? What would I do with the money?

The purpose of asking these questions isn't to judge yourself. I liken it to driving. When I drive, I know I need to stay in the correct lane or on the right side of the yellow lines, because I don't want to end up in a ditch or in front of oncoming traffic. Getting perspective helps identify whether I'm off-course and how to readjust. The only thing we have in our life is our time. It's too easy to keep your head down, work hard, and look up to discover three years have passed.

When I come home at night, my girlfriend, Rachel, often asks, "Did you have a great day?" If I say "yes," she'll want to know three things that were great about it. It puts me on the spot, but it also requires me to discover whether I'm being truthful or whether I'm wearing the mask of false optimism. As an exercise in self-assessment, I scroll through my calendar at the end of each day. For every item on my list, I ask myself if it was worth my time. Worth isn't always about money. Sometimes, it's about being in good company and having a meaningful experience.

## WHAT CAN YOU DO WITH THE INFORMATION YOU GET THROUGH PERSPECTIVE?

Developing perspective usually leads to clarity. Here are actions to consider taking based on new information:

* Make decisions based on reality.
* Figure out how to realistically keep going.
* Pivot the business if you decide you need a change.
* Create balance in your life by cultivating the personal side.
* Close the operation down if things aren't working.
* Sell your business.
* If this life isn't for you, choose to get out of entrepreneurism altogether.
* Get another job.

These actions have nothing to do with success or failure. They're personal choices. You have to stop, pause, breathe, and think about what is important to you. Use that as your guide. We're always changing; what worked one year or five years ago might not work today. People change because circumstances change. It bears repeating that being an entrepreneur is not about one job or one company so much as it is a lifestyle. Life is not static, and there's no business plan that can account for having a new baby or an ailing parent. Your life doesn't fit neatly into a business plan.

# Conclusion

—

Startups are about creating something new, and the call of the unknown and the freedom from being a corporate drone drives countless entrepreneurs. But if entrepreneurs believe and live out the urban legends embedded in startup life, they will end up creating something they hadn't anticipated: suffering. These urban legends call for you to sacrifice your well-being and your relationships. They feed the entrepreneurial obsession with nabbing a big win: going public or obtaining a lucrative exit. Yet you might reach those goals only to find out you have nothing else to show for the past three to five years that you just spent crushing it. The field of your life may be littered with broken relationships and missed opportunities to develop yourself as a person. I know because I've been there. Instagram feeds that glorify startup life with inspiring quotations and snapshots of amazing sunsets aren't telling the whole story.

Once you get a taste of entrepreneurism, however, it's tough to go back to a nine-to-five existence. If you're going to jump into entrepreneurial life, or you've decided you want (or have) to stay there, my solution is to think of yourself as a never-ending startup instead of obsessing about building the next unicorn. By doing so, you quantify happiness from a different metric. Happiness comes from the life you're living along the way. For example, I used to coach my kids' soccer team (I loved doing it; my kids not so much). Once, I had to be at a conference in Orlando the day of a game. I jumped on a plane to Atlanta just to coach it and flew right back afterward. People there were stunned I went to such lengths. My response was I wasn't going to allow being an entrepreneur to keep me from being there for the people and activities I love. Why would I stay with a job that did? The last thing I want is to spend five years focused on a startup and it alone. In those five years, I want to have traveled, spent time with my family, explored artistic pursuits, and yes, coached my kids' soccer team even though it embarrasses them to no end.

When you think of yourself as a never-ending startup, your life evolves more like an artist's does. Companies you start or run are akin to different albums, songs, or paintings. After an exit, you aren't "done." You ask yourself, "Now what?" Darius Rucker has been the lead singer for Hootie and the Blowfish for decades. That hasn't stopped him from pursuing a successful solo career as a country artist. He didn't define himself by his first success. Ben Chestnut and Dan Kurzius founded MailChimp in Atlanta during the dot-com bubble as a web design firm and evolved it into the multimillion-dollar email-marketing company it is today. As a startup, I'm an entrepreneur, speaker, author, and dad—and they're all equally important. I follow my creativity and interests when it comes to the companies I found and help. Right now, for example, I'm advising a vegan gelato company; it has nothing to do with technology, my forte, but I love the product and the people.

Many people are drawn to becoming an entrepreneur because they believe they can get rich quick. They're drawn to chasing trends: e-commerce, blockchain, multi-level marketing ("Be Your Own Boss!"). I did the same thing during the dot-com boom. Over time, I realized booms and busts come and go, and an "in-and-out" existence isn't sustainable for me to have a well-rounded and meaningful life.

My hope with this book is I've given you permission to stop being reactive, which is all too easy when you're an entrepreneur. Here are five principles that have helped me:

* No matter what the outcome, stop, pause, breathe, and think.
* Look at the totality of what you're doing over short-term results.

* Decide how you want to live.
* After you decide that, go ahead and make the changes needed.
* Go into entrepreneurship with your eyes wide open, or don't go in at all.

## CONNECTIVITY

One of the best ways for me to figure out how to design my own life is to remember I'm not a member of a startup community but of my community as a whole. When we launched our robotics company, for example, we decided to locate the office in a part of Atlanta that's considered a semi high-crime area. People criticized me for putting my employees and the space at risk for being robbed. My response was that we weren't going to be a tenant in a neighborhood but a part of it. We went door-to-door to every home and small business and invited everyone to a block party in our parking lot. One hundred and fifty people came and enjoyed burgers, hot dogs, corn hole, live music, art, and the overall crowd. It was a blast.

Every year, I host a group of young entrepreneurs from Africa who are part of the Mandela Fellowship Program, and our block party coincided with their trip. The entrepreneurs jumped into the party as if they'd been part of the neighborhood for years, socializing with everyone. Afterward, a number of them said to me, "We try so hard in our country to be part of our community, and this is the first time since we've been here that we've seen the same thing in America. We've noticed your companies don't seem to interact with your people."

The entrepreneurs from Africa are so tied to their communities because they're selling their services and products directly to the people they live with side-by-side. It's valuable for us to think the same way. Meaningful work is grounded in connectivity. One of the best ways to create both is to look up from our phones and our feeds. Meanwhile, I see it as part of my job as a global community member to help you as an entrepreneur, so feel free to visit my website (http://kpreddy.co), and drop me a line.

I'm a different person than I was when I started my startup journey years ago. I hope I've conveyed the accomplishments gained in startup life aren't what most people think going in. The accomplishments are what you learn, what you build, and how you stay in the game. You'll win some; you'll lose some. Staying in through it all takes courage. That's what being an entrepreneur is truly about.

# About the Author

**KP REDDY** has more than twenty-five years of entrepreneurship experience. He has started, grown, and sold multiple successful startups, and has been involved in building NASDAQ-listed companies and strategic acquisitions. K.P.'s work and his businesses have been featured prominently in numerous news outlets, including the *Economist*, *Huffington Post*, *Fox News*, NPR, the *Wall Street Journal*, and NBC. He is also a popular speaker at tech summits such as South by Southwest, and has advised numerous firms on innovation, from Autodesk and Mohawk Industries to Coca-Cola and UPS. K.P. lives in Atlanta, where he is the cofounder of The Combine (corporate incubator), Shadow Ventures (venture capital firm), and KP Ventures (http://kpreddy.co).